# Estimated Probabilities, Volumes, and Inundation Area Depths of Potential Postwildfire Debris Flows from Carbonate, Slate, Raspberry, and Milton Creeks, near Marble, Gunnison County, Colorado

By Michael R. Stevens, Jennifer L. Flynn, Verlin C. Stephens, and Kristine L. Verdin

Prepared in cooperation with Gunnison County

Scientific Investigations Report 2011–5047

U.S. Department of the Interior
U.S. Geological Survey

**U.S. Department of the Interior**
KEN SALAZAR, Secretary

**U.S. Geological Survey**
Marcia K. McNutt, Director

U.S. Geological Survey, Reston, Virginia: 2011

For more information on the USGS—the Federal source for science about the Earth, its natural and living resources, natural hazards, and the environment, visit http://www.usgs.gov or call 1-888-ASK-USGS

For an overview of USGS information products, including maps, imagery, and publications,
visit http://www.usgs.gov/pubprod

To order this and other USGS information products, visit http://store.usgs.gov

Suggested citation:
Stevens, M.R., Flynn, J.L., Stephens, V.C., and Verdin, K.L., 2011, Estimated probabilities, volumes, and inundation areas depths of potential postwildfire debris flows from Carbonate, Slate, Raspberry, and Milton Creeks, near Marble, Gunnison County, Colorado: U.S. Geological Survey Scientific Investigations Report 2011–5047, 30 p.

# Contents

# Figures

# Table

# Conversion Factors

SI to Inch/Pound

| Multiply | By | To obtain |
|---|---|---|
| Length | | |
| millimeter (mm) | 0.03937 | inch (in.) |
| meter (m) | 3.281 | foot (ft) |
| kilometer (km) | 0.6214 | mile (mi) |
| Area | | |
| square meter (m$^2$) | 0.0002471 | acre |
| hectare (ha) | 2.471 | acre |
| square kilometer (km$^2$) | 247.1 | acre |
| square meter (m$^2$) | 10.76 | square foot (ft$^2$) |
| hectare (ha) | 0.003861 | square mile (mi$^2$) |
| square kilometer (km$^2$) | 0.3861 | square mile (mi$^2$) |
| Volume | | |
| cubic meter (m$^3$) | 35.31 | cubic foot (ft$^3$) |
| cubic meter (m$^3$) | 1.308 | cubic yard (yd$^3$) |
| cubic meter (m$^3$) | 0.0008107 | acre-foot (acre-ft) |
| Flow rate | | |
| cubic meter per second (m$^3$/s) | 70.07 | acre-foot per day (acre-ft/d) |
| cubic meter per second (m$^3$/s) | 35.31 | cubic foot per second (ft$^3$/s) |
| Pressure | | |
| dynes per square centimeter (dynes/cm$^2$) | 0.00001450 | pounds per square inch (psi) |
| Velocity | | |
| millimeters per hour (mm/hr) | 0.03937 | inches per hour (in/hr) |

Vertical coordinate information is referenced to the North American Vertical Datum of 1988 (NAVD 88).

Horizontal coordinate information is referenced to the North American Datum of 1983 (NAD 83).

# Estimated Probabilities, Volumes, and Inundation Area Depths of Potential Postwildfire Debris Flows from Carbonate, Slate, Raspberry, and Milton Creeks, near Marble, Gunnison County, Colorado

By Michael R. Stevens, Jennifer L. Flynn, Verlin C. Stephens, and Kristine Verdin

## Abstract

During 2009, the U.S. Geological Survey, in cooperation with Gunnison County, initiated a study to estimate the potential for postwildfire debris flows to occur in the drainage basins occupied by Carbonate, Slate, Raspberry, and Milton Creeks near Marble, Colorado. Currently (2010), these drainage basins are unburned but could be burned by a future wildfire. Empirical models derived from statistical evaluation of data collected from recently burned basins throughout the intermountain western United States were used to estimate the probability of postwildfire debris-flow occurrence and debris-flow volumes for drainage basins occupied by Carbonate, Slate, Raspberry, and Milton Creeks near Marble. Data for the postwildfire debris-flow models included drainage basin area; area burned and burn severity; percentage of burned area; soil properties; rainfall total and intensity for the 5- and 25-year-recurrence, 1-hour-duration-rainfall; and topographic and soil property characteristics of the drainage basins occupied by the four creeks. A quasi-two-dimensional floodplain computer model (FLO-2D) was used to estimate the spatial distribution and the maximum instantaneous depth of the postwildfire debris-flow material during debris flow on the existing debris-flow fans that issue from the outlets of the four major drainage basins.

The postwildfire debris-flow probabilities at the outlet of each drainage basin range from 1 to 19 percent for the 5-year-recurrence, 1-hour-duration rainfall, and from 3 to 35 percent for 25-year-recurrence, 1-hour-duration rainfall. The largest probabilities for postwildfire debris flow are estimated for Raspberry Creek (19 and 35 percent), whereas estimated debris-flow probabilities for the three other creeks range from 1 to 6 percent. The estimated postwildfire debris-flow volumes at the outlet of each creek range from 7,500 to 101,000 cubic meters for the 5-year-recurrence, 1-hour-duration rainfall, and from 9,400 to 126,000 cubic meters for the 25-year-recurrence, 1-hour-duration rainfall. The largest postwildfire debris-flow volumes were estimated for Carbonate Creek and Milton Creek drainage basins, for both the 5- and 25-year-recurrence, 1-hour-duration rainfalls.

Results from FLO-2D modeling of the 5-year and 25-year recurrence, 1-hour rainfalls indicate that the debris flows from the four drainage basins would reach or nearly reach the Crystal River. The model estimates maximum instantaneous depths of debris-flow material during postwildfire debris flows that exceeded 5 meters in some areas, but the differences in model results between the 5-year and 25-year recurrence, 1-hour rainfalls are small. Existing stream channels or topographic flow paths likely control the distribution of debris-flow material, and the difference in estimated debris-flow volume (about 25 percent more volume for the 25-year-recurrence, 1-hour-duration rainfall compared to the 5-year-recurrence, 1-hour-duration rainfall) does not seem to substantially affect the estimated spatial distribution of debris-flow material.

Historically, the Marble area has experienced periodic debris flows in the absence of wildfire. This report estimates the probability and volume of debris flow and maximum instantaneous inundation area depths after hypothetical wildfire and rainfall. This postwildfire debris-flow report does not address the current (2010) prewildfire debris-flow hazards that exist near Marble.

## Introduction

Few hazards, if any, exceed the potentially devastating consequences of debris flow. Debris flows are fast-moving, high-density slurries of water, sediment, and vegetative debris with enormous destructive power that generally are triggered in response to periods of intense rainfall or, in some areas, rapid snowmelt on steep hillsides (Istanbulluoglu and others, 2004). The townsite of Marble and the surrounding area, located near the headwaters of the Crystal River in western Colorado, has been developed on two coalescing debris-flow fans (fig. 1), where damaging floods and debris flows have occurred historically (Rold and Wright, 1996). Two

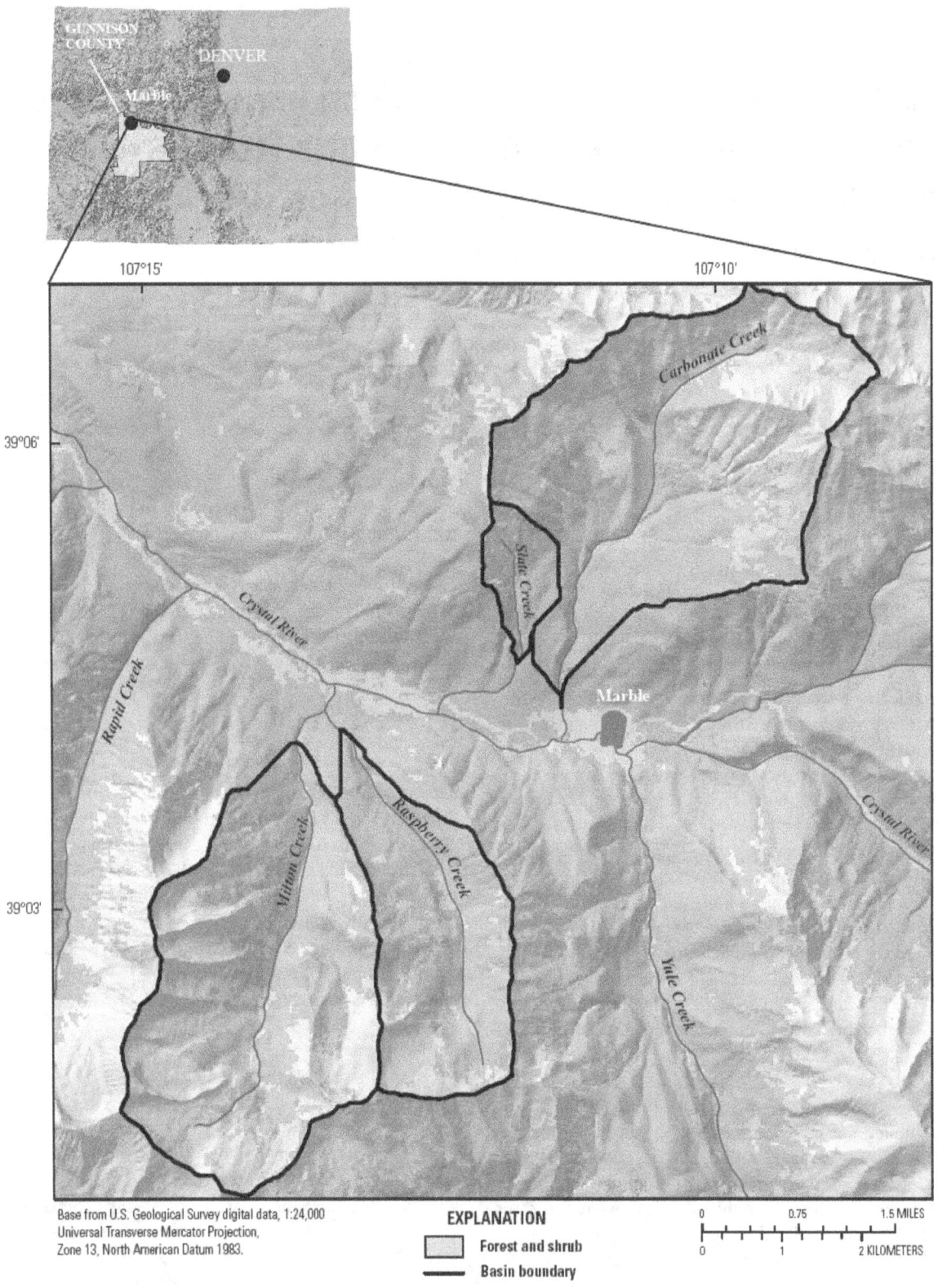

**Figure 1.**    Locations of Marble, Colorado, and Carbonate, Slate, Raspberry, and Milton Creek drainage basins.

coalescing debris-flow fans on the opposite side of the Crystal River also are being developed by landowners, and show evidence of past debris-flow activity. However, the current (2010) debris-flow potential may increase with a wildfire, likely posing greater hazards to residents, communities, infrastructure, aquatic habitat, and the water supply. Several years of drought, combined with the accelerated spread of the mountain pine beetle and fuel accumulations attributed to many years of active fire suppression, has made many forests in large areas of the Rocky Mountains increasingly susceptible to wildfire (Keane and others, 2002). Wildfires can denude hillslopes of vegetation and change soil properties that affect watershed hydrology and sediment-transport processes. Postwildfire rainfalls can cause increased overland runoff that erodes soil, rock, and vegetative debris from hillslopes (Cannon and others, 2010). Runoff reaching ephemeral stream channels may entrain stored sediment and generate hazardous debris flows (Cannon and others, 2010).

Marble is within the wildland/urban interface, where homes and businesses are interspersed with forested land at risk for wildfire. Consequently, there is a need for a hazard assessment based on estimates of the postwildfire probability of debris-flow occurrence, the volume of debris-flow material, and the potential area inundated by debris flow. During 2009, the U.S. Geological Survey (USGS), in cooperation with Gunnison County, initiated a study to identify the potential for postwildfire debris flows to occur in the Carbonate, Slate, Raspberry, and Milton Creek drainage basins near Marble, Colorado, if they are burned in a future wildfire (fig. 1). Currently (2010), these drainage basins are unburned but could be burned by a future wildfire.

Researchers currently are developing models to assess the hazards posed by postwildfire debris flows (Cannon and others, 2010; O'Brien, 2009). By considering the possible effects of a hypothetical wildfire, these models can be used to identify potential debris-flow hazards to life, property, infrastructure, and water resources before wildfires occur. It is important to recognize that large and severely burned drainage basins may produce large volumes of debris-flow material. Although the location, percentage of burned area, severity of wildfire, and storm intensity and duration after a wildfire cannot be known in advance, hypothetical or designed scenarios, such as those used in this report, are useful planning tools for conceptualizing potential postwildfire debris-flow hazards.

## Purpose and Scope

This report provides estimates of probabilities of debris-flow occurrence and the debris-flow volumes that could be generated from Carbonate, Slate, Raspberry, and Milton Creek drainage basins in response to a wildfire that burns all areas vegetated with forest and shrubs at moderate- to high-burn severity and two hypothetical postwildfire rainfalls of differing intensities. Debris-flow hydrographs defined for the estimated volumes are used as input to a model that estimates the areas

inundated by debris-flow material beyond the outlets of each drainage basin. A field reconnaissance of the Marble area to inspect debris-flow evidence and debris-flow source areas was done. Using the information provided in this report, land and water-supply managers can consider where to concentrate prewildfire planning. If a wildfire happens in the future, this information will help managers identify the drainage basins that are most vulnerable to postwildfire debris-flow hazards and the areas that could be affected by debris flows.

## Study Area

Marble, Colorado is located about 125 miles west of Denver, Colorado in Gunnison County, in the Crystal River Valley at an altitude of approximately 8,000 ft (fig. 1). Four drainage basins occupied by Carbonate, Slate, Raspberry, and Milton Creeks, tributaries to the Crystal River, are targeted in this study. The drainage basins occupied by the creeks range in size from 1.15 square kilometers ($km^2$) (0.444 $mi^2$) to 13.1 $km^2$ (5.06 $mi^2$) (table 1) and generally are forested (ESRI, 2009; Gesch and others, 2002; Homer and others, 2007). The upland vegetation consists of mixed conifer, aspen, and scrub oak, and the higher altitude parts of each drainage basin include bare rock and grass or alpine vegetation. Cretaceous sandstones and shales north of the Crystal River are overlain by alluvial deposits along the river and by colluvial deposits on adjacent valley-side hillslopes (Gaskill and Godwin, 1966; Rold and Wright, 1996). Deposits from landslides, debris flows, and rockfalls have been mapped on the north side of the Crystal River in the areas underlain by sandstone and shale (Gaskill and Godwin, 1966; Rogers and Rold, 1972; Rold and Wright, 1996). The crystalline, Tertiary-age Raspberry Creek Phacolith, which was intruded into the Cretaceous sandstones and shales, occurs in the Raspberry and Milton Creek drainage basins south of the Crystal River (Gaskill and Godwin, 1966; Rold and Wright, 1996). In the tributaries upstream from the basin outlets, surficial deposits are thin, except for landslide deposits, and generally they were not mapped by Gaskill and Godwin (1966).

## Previous Debris-Flow Hazards Investigations

Current and future development is at risk from debris flows in the Marble area, even without the occurrence of wildfires (Rold and Wright, 1996). Geomorphic hazard areas have been well described and mapped in previous investigations of the area (Rogers and Rold, 1972; Rold and Wright, 1996). Geology, topography, and erosion processes have produced a steady source of soil and rock debris, loading hillslopes and stream channels, which are susceptible to mobilization during large rainfalls. Episodic debris flows have transported large volumes of water, sediment, and debris from hillslopes and steep channels onto the debris-flow fans in the Marble area.

Debris-flow fans and debris-flow hazard areas also are mapped in detailed descriptions of geologic hazards (Rogers

**Table 1.** Debris-flow input data and estimated probability and volume at the outlets of Carbonate, Slate, Raspberry, and Milton Creeks.

[km², square kilometers; mm, millimeters; mm/hr, millimeters per hour; m³, cubic meters]

| Drainage basin | Drainage basin area (km²) | Slopes greater than 30 percent | Basin area with slopes greater than 30 percent (km²) | Basin area assumed to burn medium to high severity (km²) | Area burned medium to high severity (percent) | Basin rugged-ness | Total storm rainfall (mm) | Storm rainfall intensity (mm/hr) | Percent clay | Liquid limit (percent) | Probability of debris flow (percent) | Volume of debris flow (m³) |
|---|---|---|---|---|---|---|---|---|---|---|---|---|
| | | | | 5-year-recurrence interval, 1-hour-duration storm | | | | | | | | |
| Carbonate | 13.1 | 73 | 9.59 | 5.94 | 45 | 0.28 | 23 | 23 | 24 | 34 | 3 | 101,000 |
| Slate | 1.15 | 73 | 0.84 | 0.67 | 58 | 0.80 | 23 | 23 | 31 | 40 | 1 | 7,500 |
| Raspberry | 6.11 | 92 | 5.64 | 4.57 | 75 | 0.25 | 23 | 23 | 12 | 29 | 19 | 59,000 |
| Milton | 11.9 | 87 | 10.31 | 5.55 | 47 | 0.58 | 23 | 23 | 12 | 29 | 2 | 100,000 |
| | | | | 25-year-recurrence interval, 1-hour-duration storm | | | | | | | | |
| Carbonate | 13.1 | 73 | 9.59 | 5.94 | 45 | 0.28 | 35 | 35 | 24 | 34 | 6 | 126,000 |
| Slate | 1.15 | 73 | 0.84 | 0.67 | 58 | 0.80 | 35 | 35 | 31 | 40 | 3 | 9,400 |
| Raspberry | 6.11 | 92 | 5.64 | 4.57 | 75 | 0.25 | 35 | 35 | 12 | 29 | 35 | 74,000 |
| Milton | 11.9 | 87 | 10.31 | 5.55 | 47 | 0.58 | 35 | 35 | 12 | 29 | 5 | 125,000 |

and Rold, 1972; Rold and Wright, 1996). Debris-flow fans and runout depositional areas are prominent features located at the outlets of the four drainage basins detailed in this study. Whereas historically active debris flows have been mapped as emanating from all four drainage basins, some parts of the debris-flow fan deposits indicate little evidence of recent activity, especially the central part of the Carbonate Creek fan, which includes Marble and much of the surrounding developed area. However, the flow paths of debris flows can change as stated in a previous investigation (Rold, 1977), "… over time these channels migrate back and forth across the entire fan surface much like a fire hose gone wild." Devastating debris flows and floods have been documented in historical accounts in 1874 (reported by the Hayden Expedition), 1936, August 1941 (fig. 2, a photograph taken in 1942), July 1945, 1958, and 1972 (Rold, 1977; Rold and Wright, 1996). However, no relation between debris flows and wildfire in the area has been documented.

## Debris-Flow Susceptibility Modeling

A set of empirical equations (models) developed by Cannon and others (2010) from statistical evaluation of data collected from postwildfire debris-flow sites in the intermountain western United States were used to estimate the probability of debris-flow occurrence and estimated volumes of debris flows for the four drainage basins as a function of drainage-basin and soil characteristics, burn severity, and storm rainfall.

In past studies of wildfire-related debris-flow hazards, each drainage basin was identified by a single outlet located at the basin mouth. Conditions within the basin area above the outlet were used to estimate debris-flow probability and volume at the outlet (Cannon and others, 2007, Cannon and others, 2010). This study uses the same approach to estimate debris-flow probabilities and volumes at the outlets for each of the four drainage basins evaluated, but also advances the methodology by defining a continuous drainage network within each basin having a contributing area greater than 0.01 square kilometers, and estimating debris-flow probabilities and volumes for each 10-meter channel reach along the network. Each debris-flow probability and volume is estimated based on basin conditions within the area upstream from each channel reach. This approach provides a continuum of information within the drainage network that can be used to assess the potential debris-flow effect to existing infrastructure or yet-to-be built structures.

In recent studies, the probability and volume equations have been applied to basins that might be burned in the future by a hypothetical wildfire (Stevens and others, 2008; Elliott and others, 2011). In those studies, variables used to estimate postwildfire debris-flow probability were derived for single drainage basins and a single probability for the basin was reported. The probabilities are estimated using input variables averaged for the entire basin area and do not quantify the effects of local spatial variability. When conditions in a particular drainage basin are fairly homogeneous, the averaged model input variables such as slope, burn area, ruggedness, and soil properties are considered to be representative of the overall characteristics of the entire drainage basin. However, if the conditions in the drainage basin are heterogeneous or have a heterogeneous distribution, the averaged values of the

**Figure 2.** Aftermath of Carbonate Creek debris flow in Marble, Colorado, 1942, with Gallo Hill in the background (Photograph by Muriel Sybil Wolle used with permission from Denver Public Library Western History Department, call number X-3707).

input variables may be less representative. Using measures of variables that are averaged for an entire basin area may either underestimate or overestimate probabilities within subbasins. In hazard assessments, underestimating probability may affect public safety.

In this study, the debris-flow probability and volume estimates also were determined along the drainage network (existing flow paths or channels) using a continuous parameterization technique (Verdin and Greenlee, 2003; Verdin and Worstell, 2008). This technique was developed as an alternative to traditional basin characterization approaches, which require the selection of outlets and their corresponding basins using scientific knowledge or iterative analysis. The continuous parameterization technique also can facilitate the identification of smaller subbasins, with high probabilities for debris flow, within a larger basin. The continuous parameterization technique, based on a digital elevation model-derived flow-direction matrix, also facilitates faster parameter characterization and adds the ability to characterize basin elements above any location, not just at the major drainage-basin outlets, which provides added detail.

Using the 1/3-arc-second National Elevation Dataset digital elevation model (DEM) (Gesch and others, 2002) (10-meter nominal resolution) for the study area and the flow structure inherent in the DEM, the independent variables driving the debris-flow probability and volume equations were evaluated for every grid cell within the extent of the DEM.

Rainfall total and rainfall intensity, calculated from Miller and others (1973), were assumed to be uniform over the entire burn area because spatial differences were not sensitive in the relatively small areas of the hypothetical wildfire. Values for all of the other independent variables (except ruggedness) in the predictive equations were obtained using the continuous parameterization technique. A separate ArcGIS version 9.3 program (ESRI, 2009) was used to evaluate ruggedness for each grid cell in the study area. Once the surfaces of the independent variables were developed, the debris-flow probability and volume equations were solved using map algebra for each grid cell. Identification of the probability or volume of a debris flow at any location within the drainage basin is possible by querying the derived surfaces. For this assessment, raster sampling was used to compute the values of debris-flow probability and volume for all possible drainage-basin delineations defined by successive pour points (subbasin outlets) along existing stream channels for map areas larger than 0.01 km$^2$ (Ruddy and others, 2010).

## Debris-Flow Probability

Using a statistical evaluation of data collected from monitoring recently burned basins throughout the western United States, Cannon and others (2010) developed the following empirical equations (models) to estimate the probability of debris flow for a given drainage basin:

$$P = e^x/(1 + e^x), \qquad (1)$$

where $P$ is the probability of debris-flow occurrence in fractional form; and

$$x = -0.7 + 0.03(\%SG30) - 1.6(R) + 0.06(\%AB) + 0.07(I) + 0.2(\%C) - 0.4(LL),$$

where $\%SG30$ is the percentage of the drainage basin area with slope equal to or greater than 30 percent; $R$ is drainage basin ruggedness, the change in drainage basin elevation (meters) divided by the square root of the drainage basin area (square meters) (Melton, 1965); $\%AB$ is the percentage of drainage basin area burned at moderate to high severity; $I$ is average storm intensity (in millimeters per hour); $\%C$ is clay content of the soil (in percent); and $LL$ is the liquid limit of the soil (percentage of soil moisture by weight), which is the water content at which a soil changes from plastic to liquid behavior (Das, 1983).

## Debris-Flow Volume

Cannon and others (2010) also developed an empirical model that can be used to estimate the volume of debris flow that likely would be produced from recently burned drainage basins:

$$Ln\ V = 7.2 + 0.6(ln\ SG30) + 0.7(AB)^{0.5} + 0.2(T)^{0.5} + 0.3, \quad (2)$$

where, $V$ is the debris-flow volume, including water, sediment, and debris (cubic meters); $SG30$ is the area of drainage basin with slopes equal to or greater than 30 percent (square kilometers); $AB$ is the drainage basin area burned at moderate to high severity (square kilometers); $T$ is the total storm rainfall (millimeters); and 0.3 is a bias correction factor that changes the predicted estimate from a median to a mean value (Helsel and Hirsch, 1992). This model has an $r^2$ of 0.83 and a standard error of 0.90. In model validation, the volume equation predicted 87 percent of the debris-flow volumes within the 95-percent prediction interval (Cannon and others, 2010).

## Debris-Flow Susceptibility Model Input Data and Assumptions

Susceptibility model input data and estimated debris-flow probabilities and volumes at the outlets of Carbonate, Slate, Raspberry, and Milton Creeks were obtained from a variety of sources. Drainage basins were delineated from 10-m DEMs using tools available in ArcGIS version 9.3 (ESRI, 2009). Basin outlets were chosen from USGS 1:24,000-scale topographic maps. Drainage basin sizes ranged from 1.15 km² (0.444 mi²) to 13.1 km² (5.06 mi²) (table 1), which is within the range of drainage basin areas (0.01 to 103 km²) or (0.0039

to 39.8 mi²) used in the development of the debris-flow models (Cannon and others, 2010).

Areas covered by vegetation were used as a surrogate for areas of medium- to high-burn severity. It was assumed that all of the forest and shrub cover, which was defined from the National Land Cover Database (Homer and others, 2007), was burned at moderate- to high-burn severity within each of the drainage basins. This assumption provides a consistent basis for comparison of debris-flow hazards between drainage basins and provides a worst-case scenario for debris-flow prediction.

High-burn severity is defined by Lindsey (2002) as the complete consumption of the forest litter and duff and combustion of all fine fuels in the canopy. A deep-ash layer may be present on the forest floor, and the top layer of the mineral soil may be changed in color because of significant soil heating where large-diameter fuels were consumed. Moderate-burn severity is defined as the consumption of forest litter and duff in discontinuous patches. Leaves or needles, although scorched, may remain on trees. Foliage and twigs on the forest floor are consumed, and some heating of the mineral soils may occur if the soil organic layer was thin.

The drainage basin areas and percentage of basin areas with 30 percent or greater slopes were determined using the ArcGIS version 9.3 software (ESRI, 2009) with 10-m DEMs. Soil properties data were compiled from the State Soil Geographic (STATSGO) database (U.S. Department of Agriculture, 1991; Schwartz and Alexander, 1995). Where more than one value for clay content or liquid limit was included for a basin, a spatially weighted value was calculated. Ruggedness was computed in ArcGIS from the 10-m DEM.

Rainfall is critical to the generation of postwildfire debris flows. Post-fire debris flows studied by Cannon and others (2008 and 2010) were generated by rainfalls with recurrences ranging from less than 2 years up to 10 years. The FLO-2D-model developer recommended that the response to a 25-year rainfall also should be considered (J.S. O'Brien, FLO Engineering, Inc., oral commun., 2002). Less frequently occurring rainfall, such as the 100-year-recurrence rainfall, might deliver so much rainfall that sediment-laden water floods would be produced, rather than debris flows.

In this study, the hydrologic response to a 5-year-recurrence, 1-hour-duration rainfall of 23 mm, and a 25-year-recurrence, 1-hour-duration rainfall of 35 mm (Miller and others, 1973) was evaluated. In any given year, a 5-year-recurrence, 1-hour-duration rainfall has a 20 percent chance of occurring, and a 25-year-recurrence, 1-hour-duration rainfall has a 4 percent chance of occurring.

## Debris-Flow Inundation Modeling

To predict where postwildfire debris flows may move on the debris-flow fans at the outlets of each of the four drainage basins, two models were used. The first model is a watershed model (HEC-HMS) (U.S. Army Corps of Engineers,

2001), which is used to calibrate a hydrograph for the volume of debris-flow material estimated using the Cannon (2010) volume equation. The second model is an inundation model (FLO-2D) (O'Brien, 2009), which uses the hydrograph from the watershed model as input for modeling the downstream movement of the debris-flow material for the duration of the movement of the material downstream across the debris-flow fans. In this study, the duration of debris flow was specified as 3 hours.

## Hydrograph Estimation

Modeling the movement of debris flows across the debris-flow fans requires estimating the flow rate of debris-flow material over the period of the debris-flow occurrence (a hydrograph), which is accomplished by distributing the volume of debris-flow material, calculated from the Cannon and others (2010) volume equation through time. Rainfall, sediment concentration of the debris-flow material, and water content of the debris-flow material are estimated for each increment in a time-series over the duration of the debris-flow occurrence.

In this report, the total rainfall calculated for the 5- and 25-year, 1-hour-duration-storms, obtained from the National Oceanic and Atmospheric Administration (NOAA) Atlas 2 methods for Colorado (Miller and others, 1973), was distributed over a 1-hour period using a hyetograph, which usually is represented by a table or graph that shows what amount or what percentage of rainfall falls during each minute of the 1-hour storm. The 1-hour storm hyetograph used in this report was developed by the U.S. Army Corps of Engineers (USACE) from rainfall data in the Crystal River area (Simons, Li & Associates, Inc., 1983).

After calculating the hyetograph for each storm, the HEC-HMS watershed model (U.S. Army Corps of Engineers, 2001) was constructed using drainage-basin topographic characteristics of basin area, mean basin slope, and longest flow path in the watershed. The HEC-HMS model will distribute the rainfall over each drainage basin and compute a hydrograph for the runoff produced. HEC-HMS was implemented using the Soil Conservation Service (SCS) runoff-curve-number (RCN) method (U. S. Department of Agriculture, 1986). The SCS RCN method uses a set of equations that predict runoff from a single storm in small watersheds, taking into account water retention (surface and infiltration) (Wood and Blackburn, 1984; Sen, 2008). The SCS RCN method is consistent with empirical data used in its development, but has limitations (Grove and others, 1998; Ponce and Hawkins, 1996). For example, the SCS RCN method is not appropriate for modeling runoff with complex factors like evaporation (Sen, 2008), conditions when rainfall intensity is less than infiltration capacity (Wood and Blackburn, 1984), antecedent moisture conditions (Ponce and Hawkins, 1996), or spatial and temporal variations in curve number (Sen, 2008). Runoff-curve numbers can be estimated from vegetation, land use, and soil categories (Wood and Blackburn, 1984), and can be calibrated using runoff data or flood-peak information (Cerrelli, 2005; Livingston and others, 2005; Elliott and others, 2005; Springer and Hawkins, 2005).

To use the HEC-HMS watershed model to assist in the estimation of a hydrograph, a volume target was used to calibrate the model. Because the material represented by the hydrograph will have the water content present during the debris flow, assumptions were made to estimate the water content. For input to the inundation model, a concentration of sediment and the total volume of water and sediment must be specified (O'Brien, 2009).

The sediment concentration of the debris flow is used by the FLO-2D model to control rheological properties of the flow. These concentrations were used to develop an assumed hypothetical sedigraph estimated on the basis of results from previous studies (Pierson and Scott, 1985; Pierson and Costa, 1987; Costa, 1988; O'Brien, 2009). Sediment concentrations (Cv) used in debris-flow simulations were varied throughout the occurrence, an approach used in the Coal Seam fire and Missionary Ridge fire simulations (Elliott and others, 2005): "...initial Cv 20 percent, mean Cv approximately 31 percent, maximum Cv 48 percent, Cv 43 percent at the time of the water hydrograph peak, and Cv 20 percent for the duration [remainder] of the event." The difference in the approach used in this study is that sediment concentrations were varied during the discharge hydrograph by using a power equation to make a smooth transition from 20 percent CV at the beginning of flow and 48 percent maximum concentration at 75 percent of the time to rise to the runoff peak. Another power equation was used to estimate the decrease in sediment concentration from 48 percent to 20 percent at the end of the hydrograph. Examples of the power equations for the 25-year-recurrence, 1-hour-duration rainfall for Milton Creek are shown in figures 3 and 4.

The volume of debris-flow material estimated from Cannon and others (2010) was assumed to have a moisture content of about 20 percent (about midway between the wilting point and the field capacity of a loamy soil (International Atomic Energy Agency, 2008). This assumption was made based on the description of the way volume was estimated in the field data for the volume model (Gartner and others, 2008). For the debris-flow volume equation data, the debris-flow material was assumed to be the missing scoured material from channels or the deposited material in a fan or detention basin, which all contain some moisture prior to the time of scour, or at the time of measurement after the debris flow.

Because the FLO-2D inundation model determines rheology based on water content, additional water is then added to the Cannon and others (2010) equation volume estimate (which already includes soil moisture) to simulate the total debris-flow material water content during the flow of the material. To estimate a debris-flow volume that includes both sediment and water, the amount of water that would result in 20-percent moisture content was assumed already to be present and is then subtracted from any water content needed to

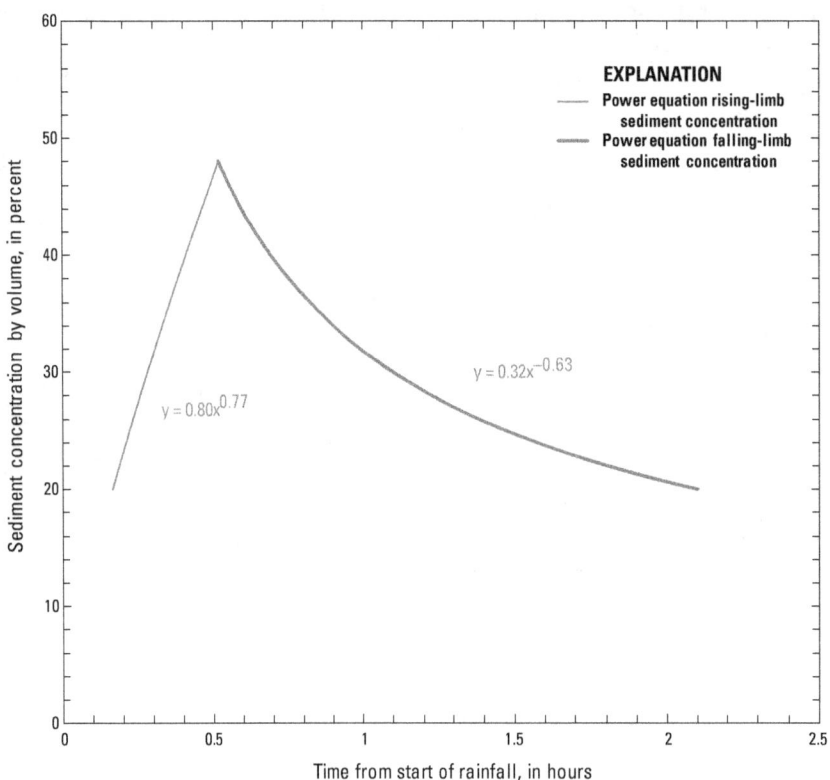

**Figure 3.** Assumed power functions used to estimate changes in sediment concentrations between starting, peak, and ending sediment concentrations for the debris-flow inundation simulation (the 25-year-recurrence, 1-hour-duration rainfall case for the Milton Creek drainage basin shown here).

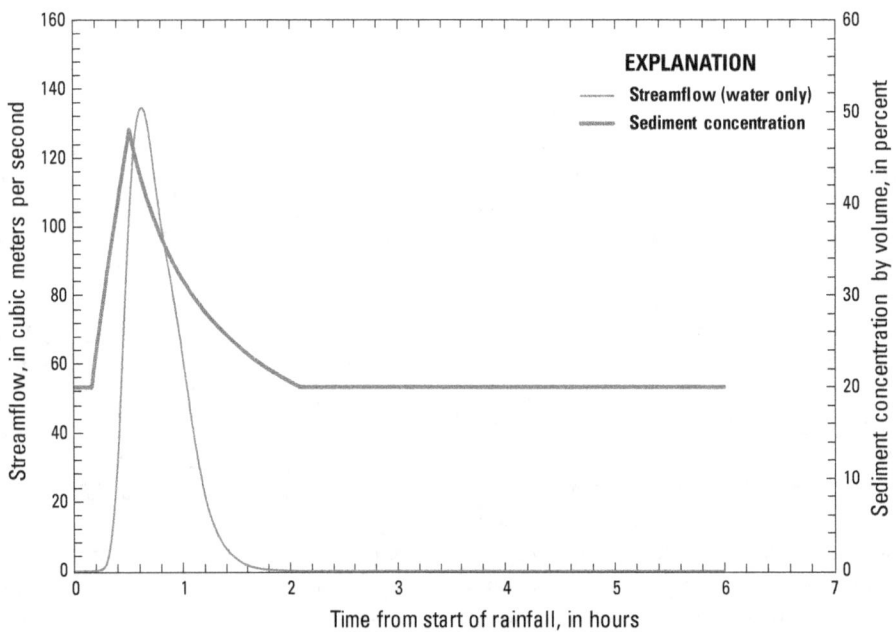

**Figure 4.** Estimated hydrograph of streamflow (water only) and debris-flow sediment concentration with time for the simulation of the 25-year-recurrence, 1-hour-duration rainfall in the Milton Creek drainage basin.

bulk up the material to represent the sediment concentration during the debris flow. During the debris flow, the material has the initial soil moisture content prior to being scoured plus the water from rainfall runoff that entrained that material. Thus, the debris-flow volume equation is bulked to simulate the water content minus the initial moisture content. For example, if the concentration of sediment in the debris flow is assumed to be 45 percent at an instantaneous time increment during the runoff, the flow material contains an assumed 20-percent water content (soil moisture) from the equation volume, and another 25-percent water content to get the sediment concentration to the assumed value. The 25-percent proportion of water is bulked and added to the equation volume.

The next step is to calibrate the hydrograph to the bulked volume estimate. First, a range of assumed Runoff Curve Numbers (RCNs) were input to the HEC-HMS model. Then, by using an iterative procedure, the HEC-HMS time-series distribution (hydrograph) of the volume that was closest to the volume predicted by the bulked equation was used in the FLO-2D inundation model.

## Inundation Model Implementation

The FLO-2D inundation model used for this study is a Federal Emergency Management Agency approved two-dimensional computer model capable of simulating channel, overbank, and unconfined flooding on an alluvial fan, such as the relict debris-flow fans downstream from the basin outlets (O'Brien, 2009). To estimate the potential inundation from water and debris in response to a hypothetical postwildfire storm, the hydrograph produced in HEC-HMS was used as input to the FLO-2D model (O'Brien, 2009) to develop estimates of inundation downstream from the drainage basin outlets of Carbonate, Slate, Milton, and Raspberry Creeks (fig. 1). Results from FLO-2D modeling provide spatial estimates of maximum instantaneous inundation depths that occur during the debris flow.

The FLO-2D model (O'Brien, 2009) is a quasi-two-dimensional hydraulic model that simulates unconfined spread of material (water, sediment, and debris) on debris-flow fans and valley bottoms. The FLO-2D model has previously been used to estimate postwildfire inundation in Colorado (Elliott and others, 2005). FLO-2D also was used in Yosemite National Park to simulate debris flows using field evidence to calibrate the model (Bertolo and Wieczorek, 2005). The model uses a specified input hydrograph, volumetric sediment concentration, existing topography, and roughness estimates to route a debris flow from the basin outlet of the originating tributary to the depositional area on the debris-flow fan.

Unconfined flow is allowed in eight directions (quasi-two-dimensional) through each grid cell (the four sides and four corners of a square, quasi-two-dimensional). The model accepts a user-defined hydrograph and variable time-steps are automatically regulated by the model using wave-celerity and Froude-number limits. FLO-2D simulates flood-wave attenuation and ground-surface detention. Volume-conservation and any unreasonable flow velocities computed by the model are monitored by the user as a quality-assurance measure (O'Brien, 2009).

For implementation of the FLO-2D model in the Marble area drainage basins, 10 meter (100 m² grid) DEMs were used to define the topographic flow surface (debris-flow channel and fan deposition zones) onto which the debris flows generated in the upper basin would be discharged. After preliminary runs of the model it was discovered that the results were not sensitive to differences of scale. The final model was gridded to 20-meters (400-m² grid cells) within the preprocessor for the FLO-2D model. Other assumptions are needed for the model simulation of debris flows. Infiltration and evaporative losses were assumed to be zero. The initial Manning's roughness coefficient was assumed to be 0.07, but within the model the roughness increases if the velocity increases such that the limit of 0.99 set for the Froude number is exceeded. The limit restrained the model run to a subcritical flow regime only, which is a reasonable assumption considering the turbulence and shallow depth in these channels. Channel and floodplain scour and deposition were not simulated in the model.

The hydrograph (previously explained in the "Hydrograph Estimation" section of this report) was assigned to an inflow point just upstream from the apex of each alluvial fan that corresponds to the outlet of each of the four drainage basins. Putting the debris-flow discharge into the model upstream from the fan apex allowed the modeled flow to adjust and stabilize after abrupt input at the inflow point before discharging onto the fan.

Yield stress and viscosity in the FLO-2D model are the primary controlling factors for rheology of the debris flows, along with sediment concentration. Yield stress generally describes "the threshold strength…which must be exceeded for motion to occur" (Enos, 1977) and generally relates to particle friction properties. Viscosity generally describes the visco-plastic properties of the sediment-water mixture, which relate to pore fluid pressures (small grain-size effect) (Kaitna and others, 2007). Viscosity exerts more control on debris-flow runout distances when yield strength is low (Elverhoi and others, 2000); yield strength, when relatively high, controls runout distance more than viscosity. Flood discharges that were bulked for debris-flow sediment concentrations (previously detailed in the "Hydrograph Estimation" section of this report) need additional sediment properties to be assumed before running the model. The rheological properties of the debris-flow material in O'Brien and Julien (1988) were chosen from experimental soil data characterizing soils found in the Glenwood Springs and Aspen areas of Colorado, located 22 miles north and 34 miles northeast of Marble. Two soils were chosen from O'Brien and Julien (1988) to represent soils in the Marble area for the simulation. The "Aspen natural soil," which has a clay percentage equal to 27.5 (O'Brien and Julien, 1988), best represents soils eroded from the shales of Carbonate and Slate Creeks, which have clay percentages equal to 24 and 31, respectively (STATSGO data: U.S.

Department of Agriculture, 1991). The "Glenwood sample 4" soil (O'Brien and Julien, 1988), which has a clay percentage equal to 7.6 percent, is the soil that best represents the clay content of material derived from the phacolith that characterizes the geology of the Raspberry Creek and Milton Creek drainage basins, which have a clay percentage of 12 percent. Yield stress of the Aspen natural and Glenwood sample 4 soils are $3.83 \times 10^{-2}$ and $1.72 \times 10^{-3}$ dynes per square centimeter, respectively (with beta coefficients 19.6 and 29.5, respectively) (O'Brien and Julien, 1988). Viscosity of the Aspen natural and Glenwood sample 4 soils are $4.95 \times 10^{-3}$ and $6.02 \times 10^{-4}$ dynes per square centimeter, respectively (with beta coefficients 27.1 and 33.1, respectively) (O'Brien and Julien, 1988).

The FLO-2D model was used to simulate 3 hours of debris-flow movement (the length of time for most of the material to cross the debris-flow fans in the simulation). An inundation area produced from the FLO-2D output showed the debris-flow inundation and maximum instantaneous depth attained in the flow path on each relict debris-flow fan below the outlet in each of the four drainage basins.

# Estimated Probabilities, Volumes, and Inundation Area Depths of Potential Postwildfire Debris Flows

The following three sections present the results of the study. It is important to recognize that the results are based on equations and models applied in hypothetical postwildfire and rainfall scenarios, and the estimates need to be considered within that uncertainty.

## Debris-Flow Probabilities

Estimated debris-flow probabilities calculated from drainage-basin characteristics identified for the entire basin area at the outlets of the four drainage basins ranged from 1 to 19 percent in response to the 5-year-recurrence, 1-hour-duration rainfall, and ranged from 3 to 35 percent in response to the 25-year-recurrence, 1-hour-duration rainfall (table 1). Conditions in Raspberry Creek produced the highest probabilities (19 and 35 percent), whereas probabilities estimated for Carbonate, Slate, and Milton Creeks were similar and ranged from 1 to 6 percent for both rainfall scenarios. It is not clear why the highest probabilities are associated with Raspberry Creek, but of the four drainage basins, Raspberry Creek has the largest percentage of area burned (table 1). For the 4 drainage basins, the 25-year-recurrence, 1-hour-duration rainfall debris-flow probabilities are 2 to 3 times higher than for the 5-year-recurrence, 1-hour-duration rainfall.

When the debris-flow probability model was implemented continuously along the drainage basin stream networks (figs. 5-8) many stream channels within the 4 drainage basins

show debris-flow probabilities greater than 10 percent (see the colored points along the streams) and a few channels in the Raspberry Creek drainage basin show debris-flow probabilities exceeding 40 percent (fig. 7), which indicates that some stream channels may be more susceptible to postwildfire debris flow than others. As expected, the estimated postwildfire debris-flow probabilities are greater in response to the 25-year-recurrence, 1-hour-duration rainfall than to the 5-year-recurrence, 1-hour-duration rainfall (figs. 5-8). In the Carbonate, Slate, and Milton drainage basins (figs. 5, 6, and 8), only a few locations in each basin indicate probabilities greater than 10 percent in response to either the 5- or 25-year-recurrence, 1-hour-duration rainfalls. Results for the Raspberry Creek drainage basin considering the 25-year-recurrence, 1-hour-duration rainfall, indicate widespread areas with postwildfire probabilities of debris-flow occurrence greater than 10 percent, and many areas with probabilities greater than 20 percent (fig. 7).

## Debris-Flow Volumes

Estimated postwildfire debris-flow volumes are proportional to the drainage area burned. Debris-flow volumes estimated at the outlets of the four drainage basins (table 1) for the 5- and 25-year-recurrence, 1-hour-duration rainfalls were, respectively: Carbonate Creek 101,000 and 126,000 $m^3$; Slate Creek 7,500 and 9,400 $m^3$; Raspberry Creek 59,000 and 74,000 $m^3$; and Milton Creek 100,000 and 125,000 $m^3$. Carbonate and Milton Creeks had the largest estimated volumes (primarily a function of larger basin areas). These results indicate that generally, the 25-year-recurrence, 1-hour-duration rainfall increases debris-flow volume at the drainage basin outlet by about 25 percent in comparison to the 5-year-recurrence, 1-hour-duration rainfall.

The postwildfire debris-flow volume estimates also were made using the same continuous parameterization technique that was used to estimate postwildfire debris-flow probability. The results for the four drainage basins (figs. 9-12) generally indicate that volume of water and sediment increased as contributing drainage area increased. Because all the coefficients for the variables are positive, and burned area (potentially the strongest variable in the equation) never decreases as contributing drainage area is added in the downstream direction, progressively larger debris-flow volumes are estimated.

It is important to understand that the individual colored points shown in the figures are estimated debris-flow volumes at that point. An incorrect interpretation would be that successive grid volume estimates are cumulative downstream. The volume maps may be useful for interpolating debris-flow volumes at a particular point along a stream channel or for understanding the amount of debris-flow material that could be expected to pass through any location in the subbasins.

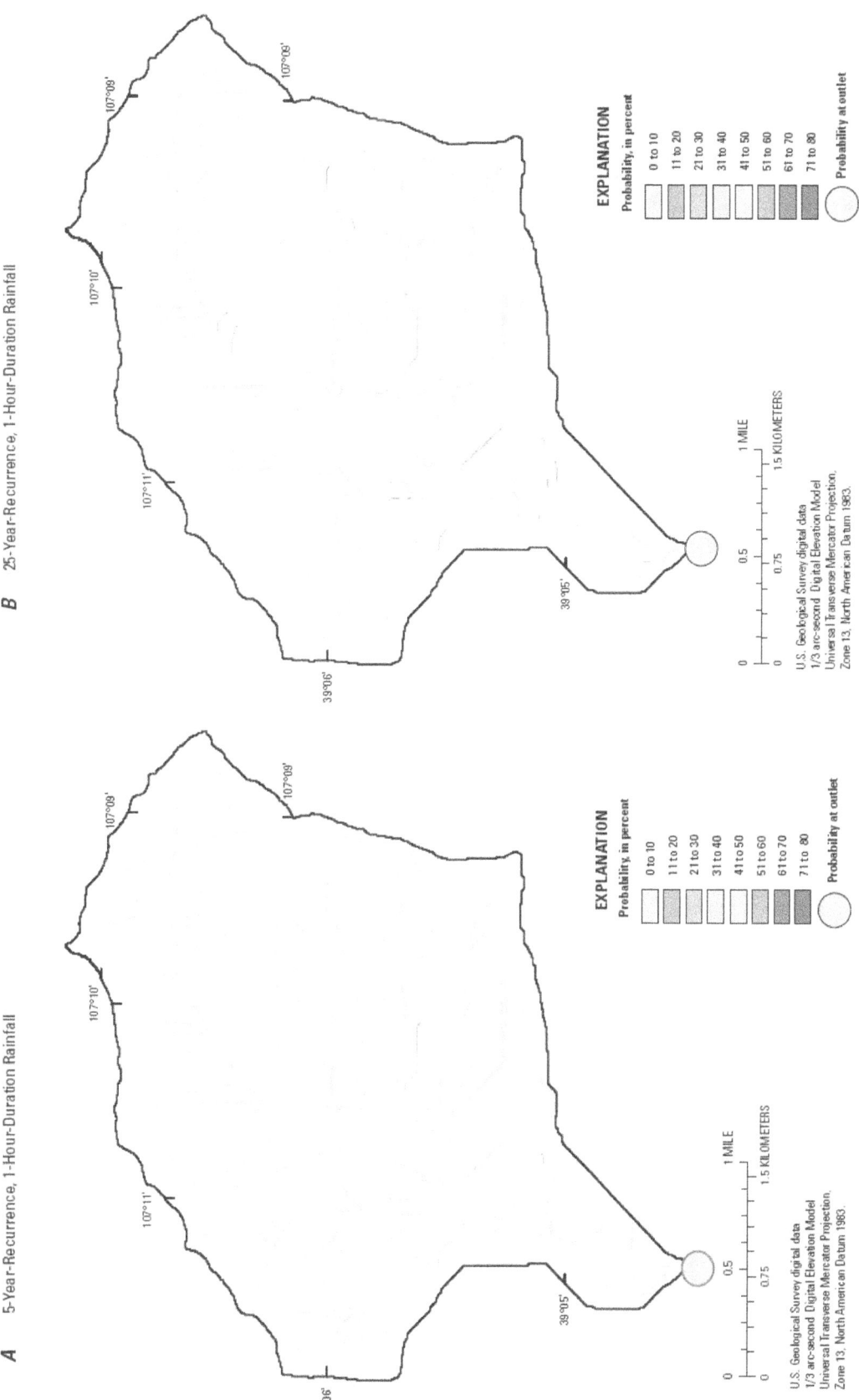

**Figure 5.** Probability of debris flow estimated for stream channels and flow paths in the Carbonate Creek drainage basin in response to the (*A*) 5-year-recurrence, 1-hour-duration rainfall, and (*B*) 25-year-recurrence, 1-hour-duration rainfall.

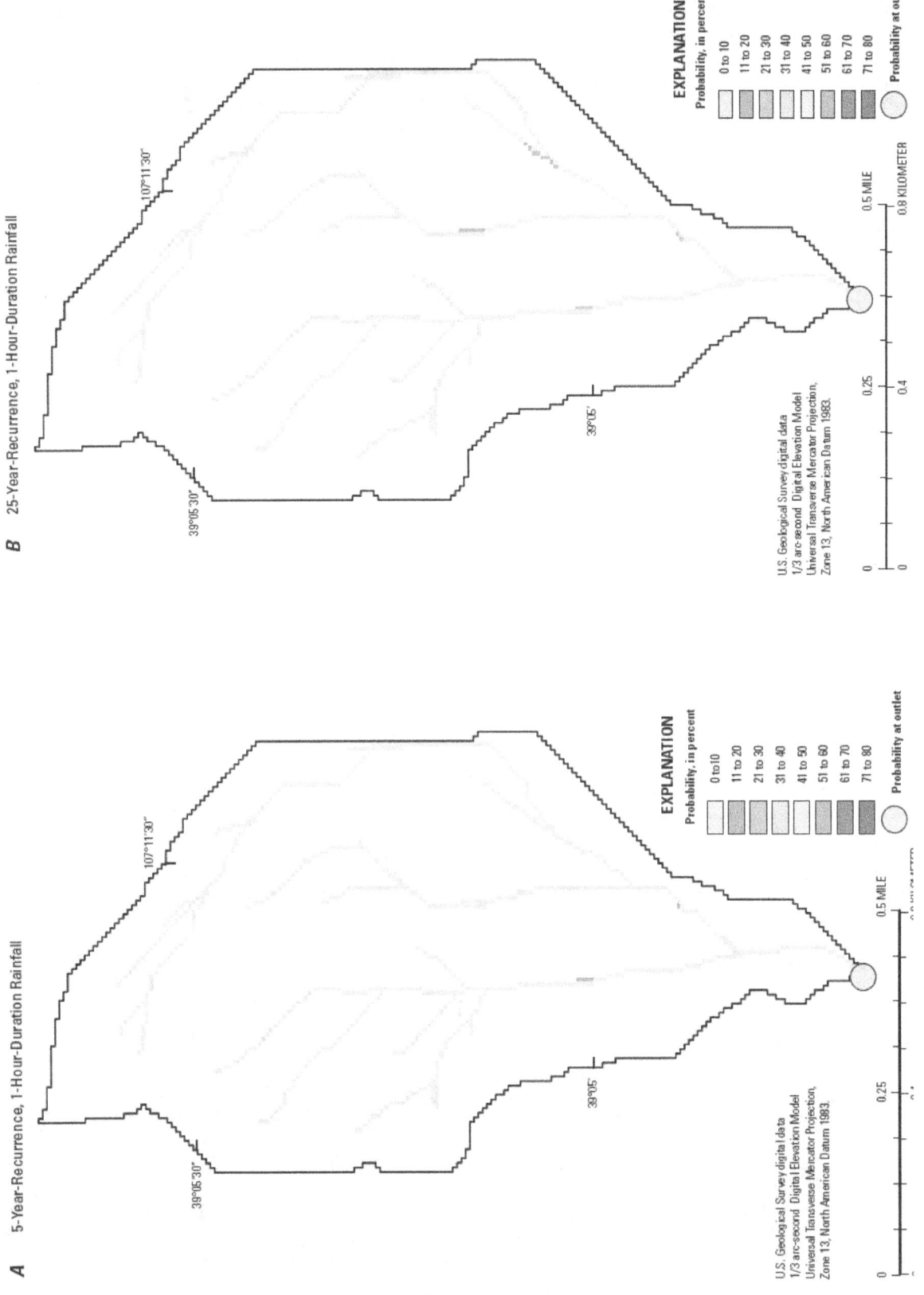

**Figure 6.**    Probability of debris flow estimated for stream channels and flow paths in the Slate Creek drainage basin in response to the (A) 5-year-recurrence, 1-hour-duration rainfall, and (B) 25-year-recurrence, 1-hour-duration rainfall.

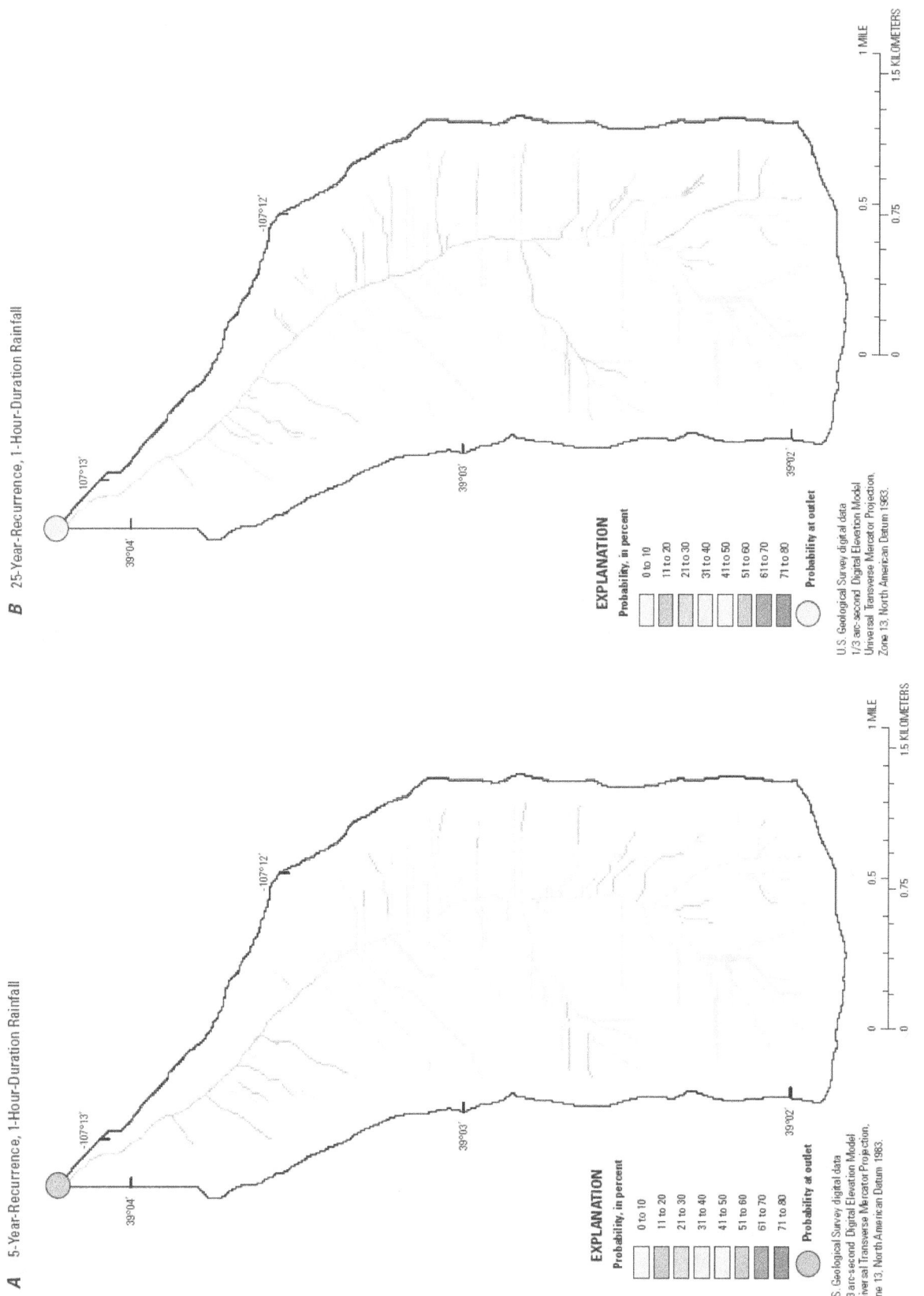

**Figure 7.** Probability of debris flow estimated for **stream channels and flow paths** in the Raspberry Creek drainage basin in response to the (*A*) 5-year-recurrence, 1-hour-duration rainfall, and (*B*) 25-year-recurrence, 1-hour-duration rainfall.

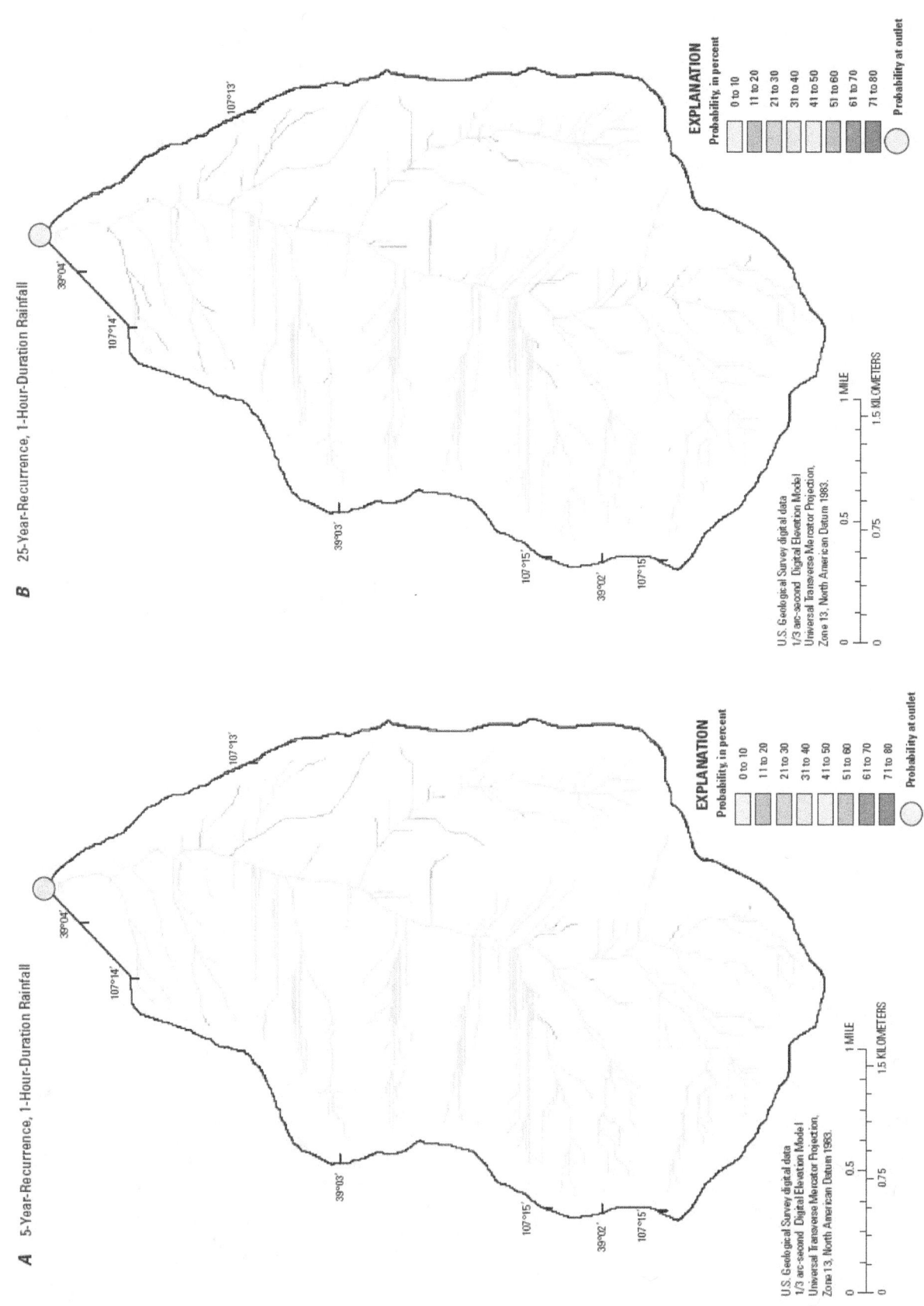

**Figure 8.** Probability of debris flow estimated for stream channels and flow paths in the Milton Creek drainage basin in response to the (*A*) 5-year-recurrence, 1-hour-duration rainfall, and (*B*) 25-year-recurrence, 1-hour-duration rainfall.

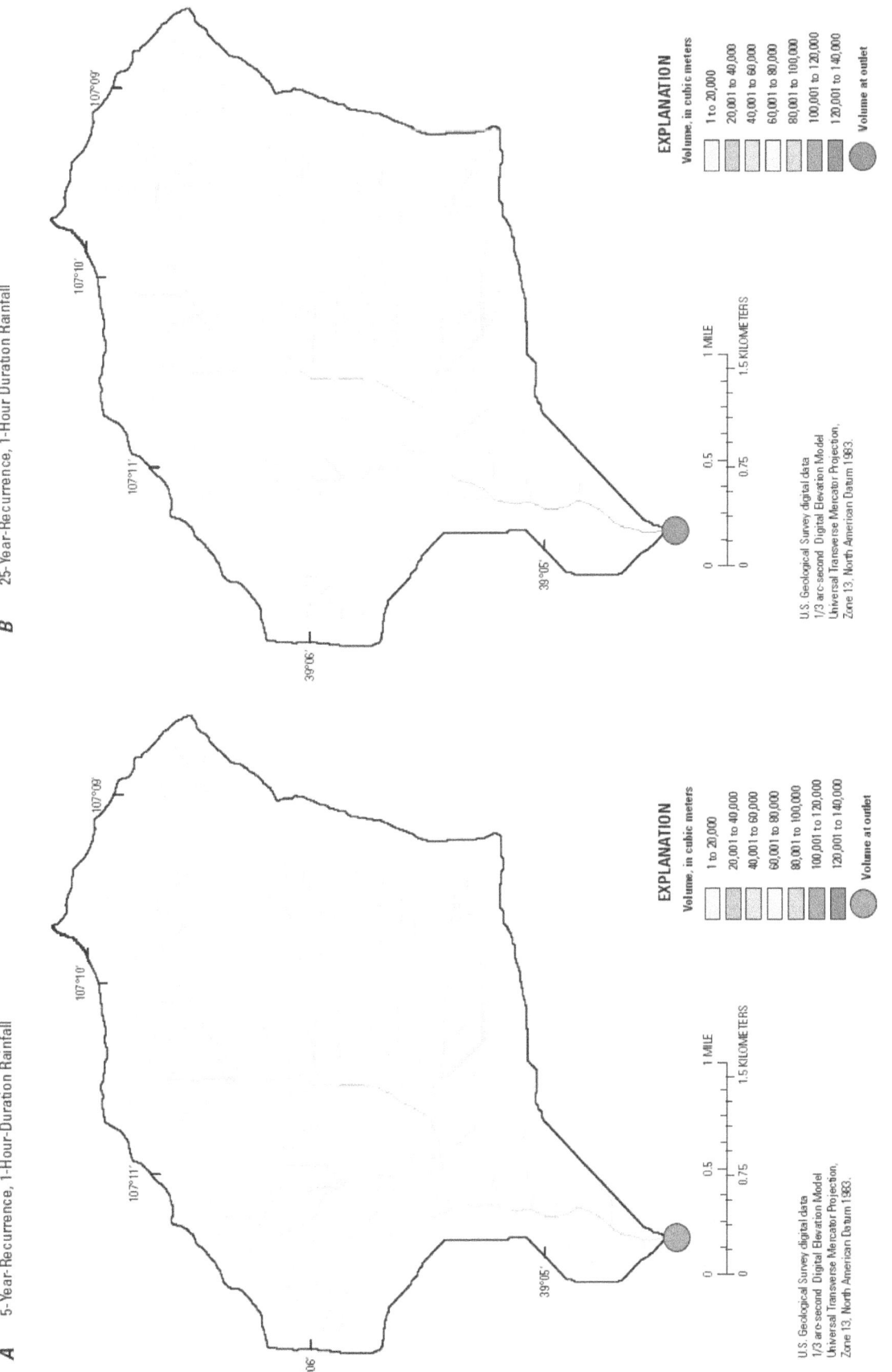

**Figure 9.** Volume of debris flow estimated for stream channels and flow paths in the Carbonate Creek drainage basin in response to the (*A*) 5-year-recurrence, 1-hour-duration rainfall, and (*B*) 25-year-recurrence, 1-hour-duration rainfall.

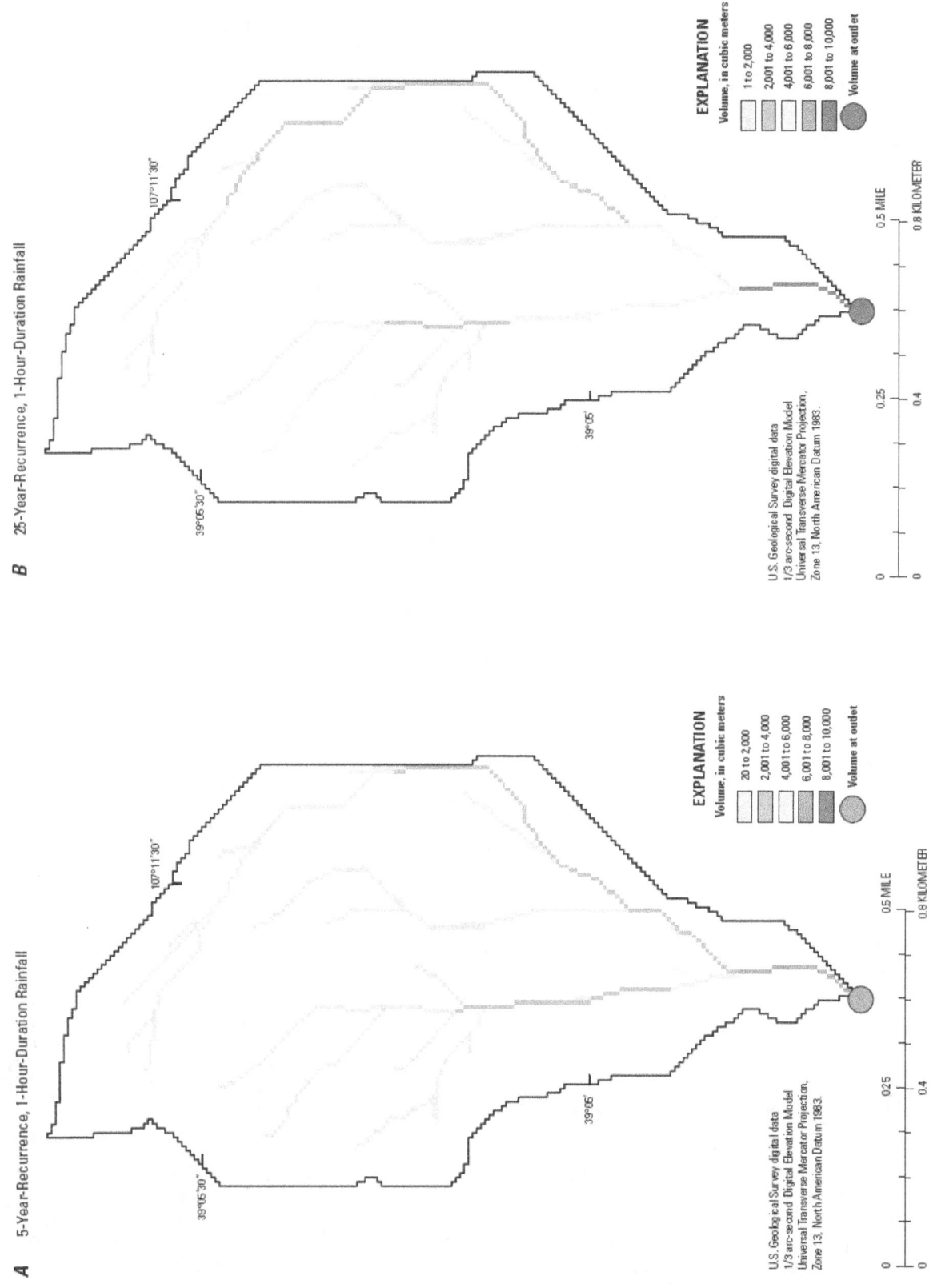

**Figure 10.**    Volume of debris flow estimated for stream channels and flow paths in the Slate Creek drainage basin in response to the (*A*) 5-year-recurrence, 1-hour-duration rainfall, and (*B*) 25-year-recurrence, 1-hour-duration rainfall.

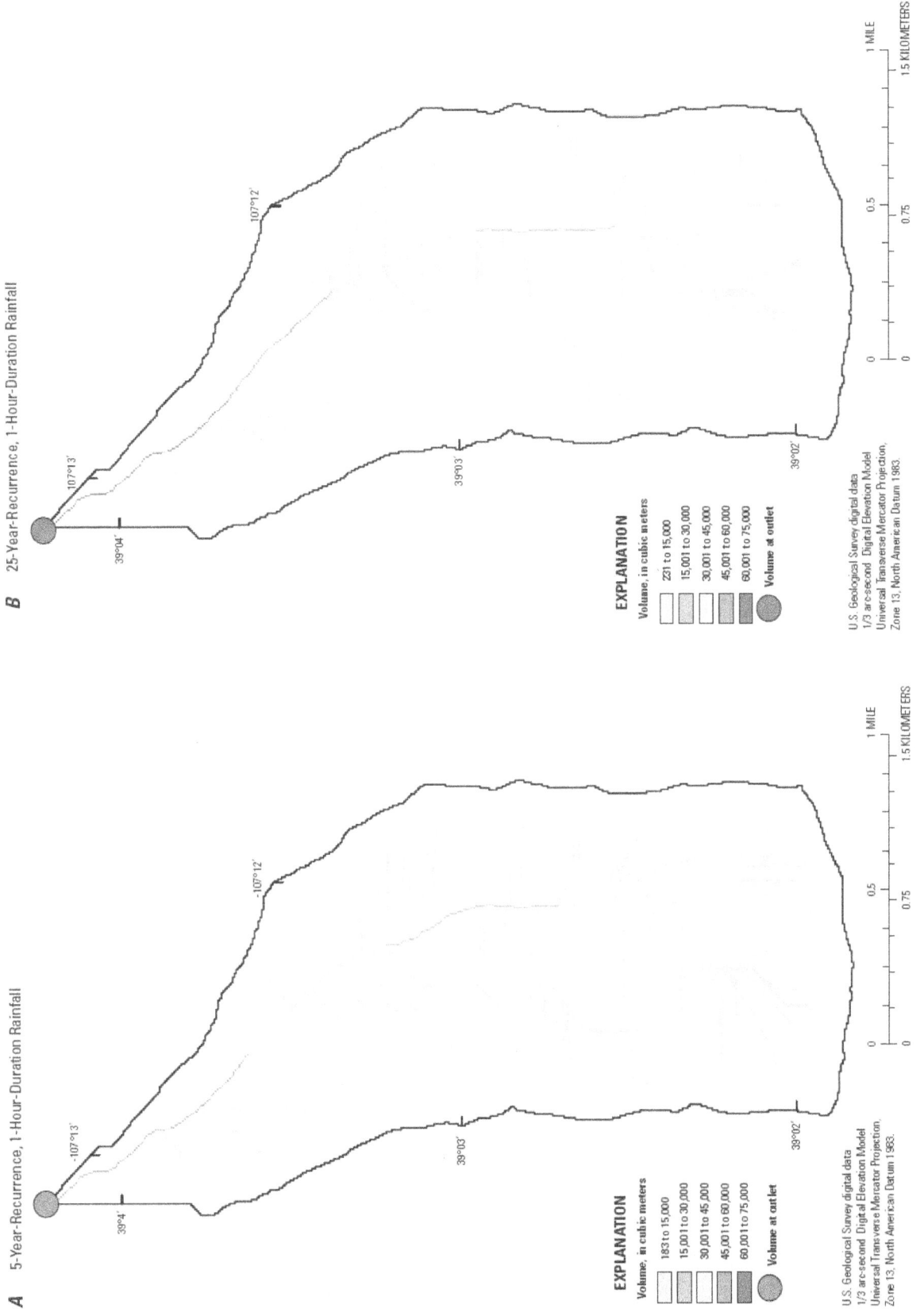

**Figure 11.**   Volume of debris flow estimated for stream channels and flow paths in the Raspberry Creek drainage basin in response to the (*A*) 5-year-recurrence, 1-hour-duration rainfall, and (*B*) 25-year-recurrence, 1-hour-duration rainfall.

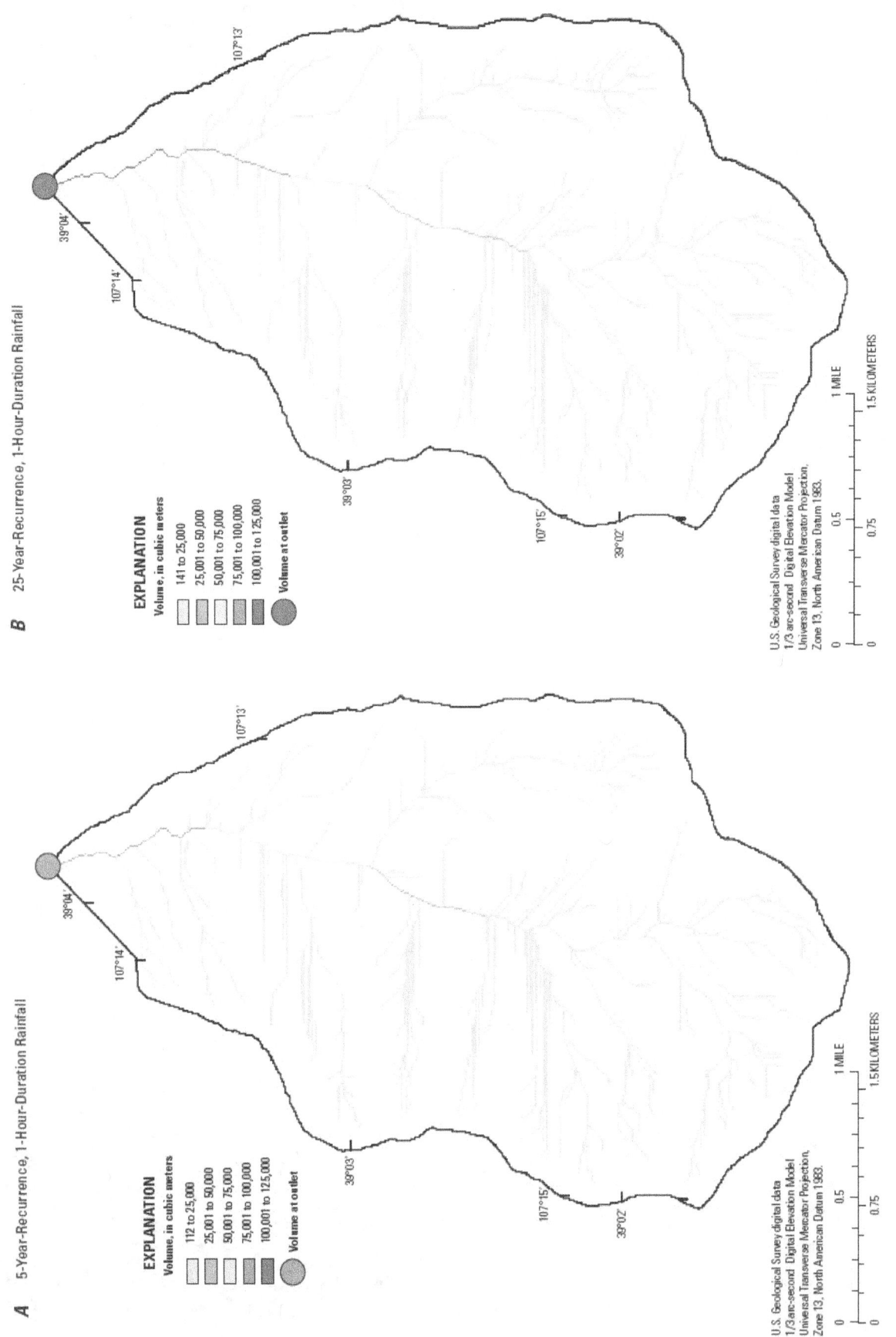

**Figure 12.** Volume of debris flow estimated for stream channels and flow paths in the Milton Creek drainage basin in response to the (A) 5-year-recurrence, 1-hour-duration rainfall, and (B) 25-year-recurrence, 1-hour-duration rainfall.

## Debris-Flow Inundation Area Depths

Results of the FLO-2D inundation modeling of the 5- and 25-year-recurrence, 1-hour duration rainfalls after a hypothetical wildfire indicate that postwildfire debris flows below the drainage-basin outlets of Carbonate, Raspberry, and Milton Creeks would flow all the way to the Crystal River. The postwildfire debris flow from Slate Creek would nearly reach the Crystal River in response to the 5-year recurrence, 1-hour duration rainfall, and would reach the river in response to the 25-year-recurrence, 1-hour duration rainfall. The FLO-2D model results indicate that simulated postwildfire debris flows of the magnitude predicted in this study utilize pre-existing stream channels and flow paths caused by prior floods or debris flows. The model results are similar to the hazard areas (fig. 13, red outline) delineated by Rogers and Rold (1972) and Rold and Wright (1996) (fig. 13, blue outline). The current (2010) study provides estimates of debris-flow inundation area and depth for a defined rainfall under a postwildfire soil condition, which is not representative of the unburned conditions in the drainage basins. The inundation area predicted in the current (2010) study is somewhat larger and more elongated than the mudflow and hazard zones mapped by Rogers and Rold (1972), and the debris-flow areas mapped by Rold and Wright (1996). The smaller active debris-flow areas mapped by Rold and Wright (1996) may be the result of a debris flow from a smaller runoff response than those assumed in this report, or from features on the ground that would otherwise restrict or alter the debris flow but that may not have been captured by the 10-meter DEM topography. Rold and Wright (1996) mapped areas in Marble that they considered not in "recent or active debris-flow" areas and adjacent areas that could be considered for development with "site specific study for risk assessment." There is much uncertainty with respect to the postwildfire debris-flow hazard associated with larger storm events than were considered in this study, such as the 100-year-recurrence rainfall, and caution is needed.

One potential problem with using recent debris-flow activity as a hazard indicator is that the debris-flow channels may get blocked and large debris flows could greatly exceed channel capacity, which could change the course of a debris flow or cause a debris flow to reoccupy a previously inactive channel or deposition zone. Rogers and Rold (1972) mapped and described a diversion point on Slate Creek where the channel was altered to its present course, which is away from the channel that historically inundated part of the larger relict debris-flow fan located just east of Slate Creek (flow path on figure 13). Rogers and Rold (1972) states, "According to local reports, this channel was artificially plugged and diverted to its present course by Marble residents to prevent Slate Creek mudflows from entering the town." This vulnerable diversion point could be changed again during a large debris flow and may cause inundation on a currently inactive portion of the fan.

Estimated postwildfire debris-flow material exceeded depths of 5 meters during the debris flow in some areas (fig. 13). These depths are the maximum-attained instantaneous depth during the debris flow, not the remnant depth of material when the debris flow stops. Comparing results of the 5- and 25-year-recurrence interval, 1-hour-duration rainfalls, only small differences in the inundation areas and depths of debris-flow material were estimated by the FLO-2D model (fig. 13). Existing stream channels or topographic flow paths seem to control the distribution of debris-flow material, and the 25-percent larger debris-flow volume estimated for the 25-year-recurrence, 1-hour-duration rainfall compared to the 5-year-recurrence, 1-hour-duration rainfall does not seem to substantially affect the areal distribution of debris-flow material.

Predicted maximum instantaneous depths of debris-flow material along the channel of the Crystal River need to be considered coarse estimates because the dilution of the debris-flow sediment concentration from water in the Crystal River is not simulated by the FLO-2D modeling, and less concentrated sediment mixtures could exhibit different behavior. Also, blockages by coarse debris such as trees, houses, vehicles, and large boulders might alter the debris flow paths or the channel of the Crystal River; blockages were not simulated in this study.

## Field Reconnaissance

USGS identified geomorphic evidence of past debris flows on the debris-flow fans and in the stream channels downstream from the outlets of each of the four drainage basins. The current (2010) unburned source area for debris flows in Carbonate and Slate Creeks are the shale and sandstone exposures on Gallo Hill and the relatively barren side slopes of incised gullies and channels (fig. 14). A large wildfire would expose areas, which are currently (2010) covered by woody vegetation in Carbonate and Slate Creeks as well as similar areas in Raspberry and Milton Creeks, to the erosive effects of rainfall. Carbonate Creek flows through an area of historic debris flows that exhibit debris-flow levees (Costa and Jarrett, 1981) and a braided stream channel that is indicative of an abundant sediment supply (fig. 15). Slate Creek is an active debris-flow drainage basin with obvious debris-flow runout zones (figs. 16 and 17), and in 2008 a relatively small debris flow destroyed a home near Slate Creek (fig. 18).

The likely source areas for debris flows in Milton and Raspberry Creeks are the steep, actively eroding hillslopes within the drainage basins (fig. 19). A wildfire on these slopes would further expose the area to rainfall and erosion, providing material for debris flows. Raspberry and Milton Creeks have terminal relict debris-flow fans and lateral debris-flow levees (Costa and Jarrett, 1981) that are well developed but do not show much evidence of recent overbank debris flow that exceeded the capacity of the existing channel (figs. 20-23). However, large debris flows from these drainage basins could cause substantial flooding if they were to block the Crystal River.

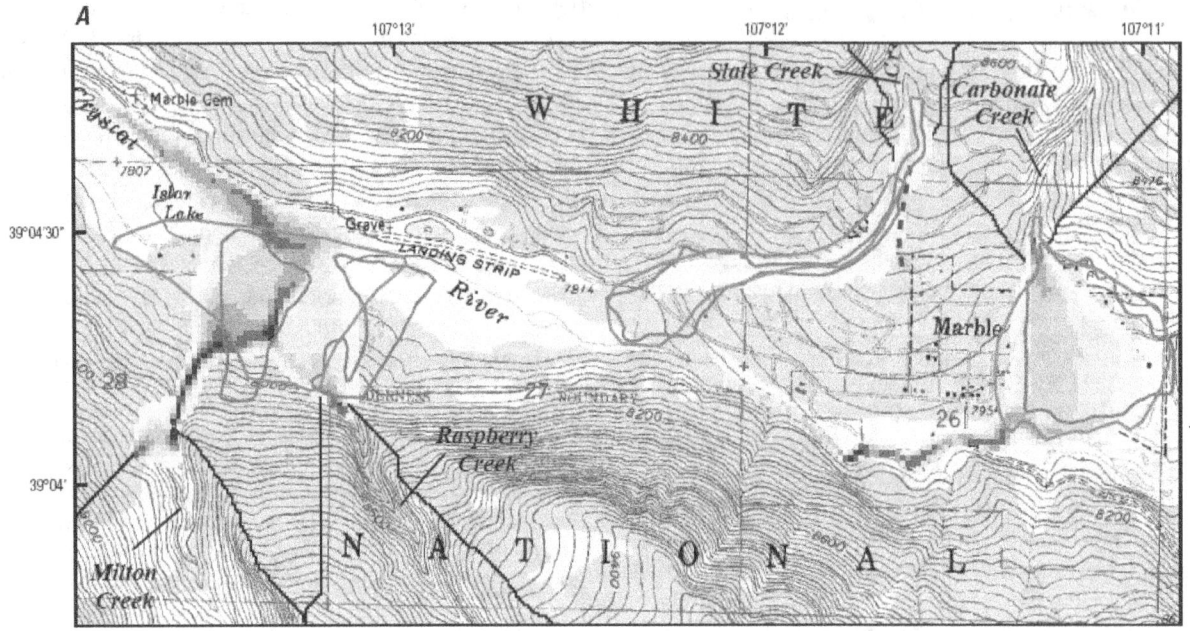

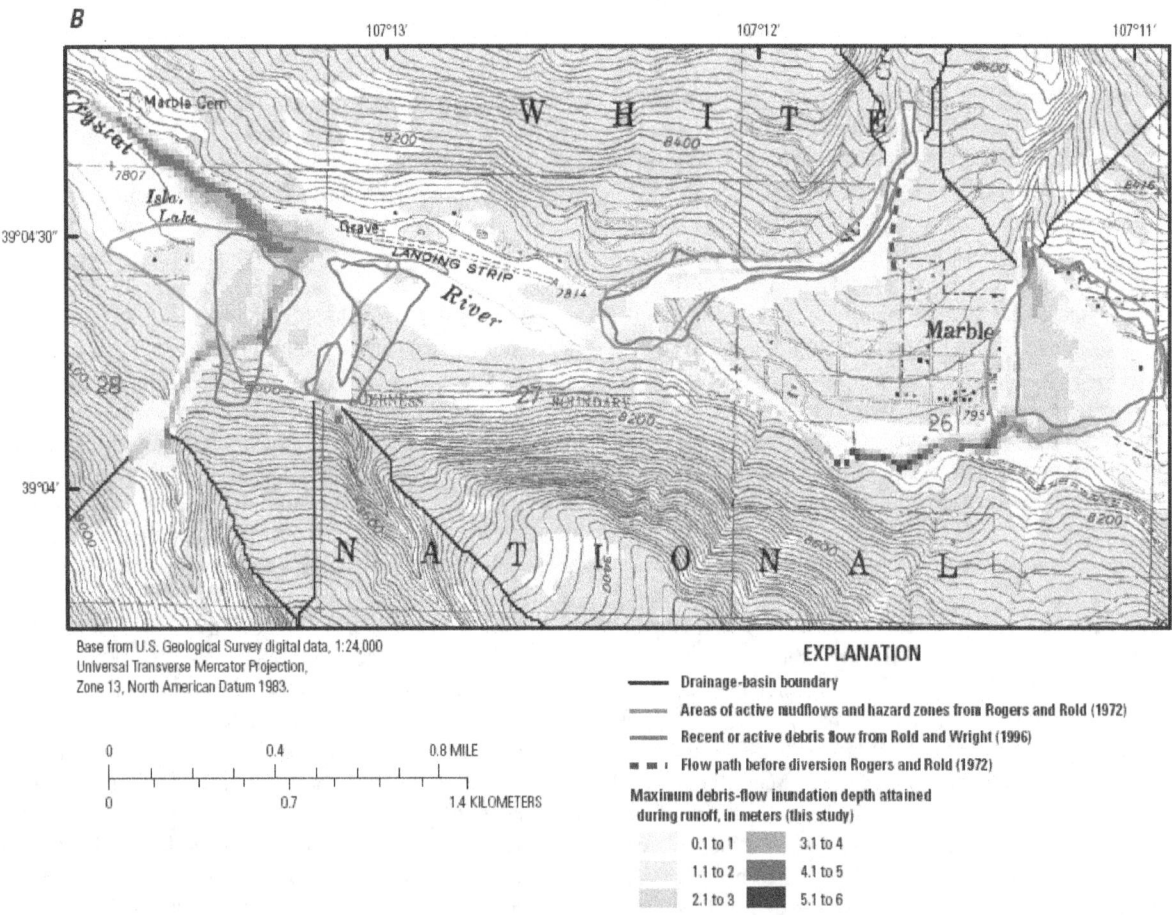

**Figure 13.** Contour map showing debris-flow inundation depths estimated for the debris-flow volumes generated in reponse to the (*A*) 5-year-recurrence, 1-hour-duration rainfall, and (*B*) 25-year-recurrence, 1-hour-duration rainfall at Carbonate, Slate, Raspberry, and Milton Creek drainage basins.

**Figure 14.** Gallo Hill, at the head of Slate Creek in June 2008, a source area for prewildfire debris-flow material.

**Figure 15.** Carbonate Creek (view south, downstream) just upstream from the confluence with the Crystal River in June 2008, showing the braided stream confined by debris-flow levees on both banks (Photograph taken by Mike Stevens, U.S. Geological Survey).

**Figure 16.** Debris-flow deposits on Slate Creek just east of Marble, Colorado, in July 2008. Blocks of Yule Marble on the left (Photograph taken by Mike Rupert, U.S. Geological Survey).

**Figure 17.** Debris-flow deposits on Slate Creek (showing cobble and boulder-sized material supported in a fine grained matrix) west of Marble, Colorado, in July 2008, just upstream from the confluence with the Crystal River. Deposits were incised during recession of the debris flow or by the stream after the debris flow (Photograph taken by Mike Rupert, U.S. Geological Survey).

**Figure 18.** Home destroyed by debris flow on Slate Creek, July 2008 (Photograph taken by Mike Rupert, U.S. Geological Survey).

## Limitations and Uncertainties

This report provides estimates of potential debris-flow probability, volume, and debris-flow inundation downstream from areas assumed to be burned by a hypothetical wildfire in response to 5- and 25-year-recurrence, 1-hour-duration rainfalls. The estimated postwildfire debris-flow hazards likely are most significant 1 to 3 years following wildfire (Cannon and others, 2007). The 5-year-recurrence, 1-hour-duration rainfall is more likely to occur than the 25-year-recurrence, 1-hour-duration rainfall, and at the time when the burned area is most vulnerable to debris flows and floods. Response to a 25-year-recurrence, 1-hour-duration rainfall illustrates a less likely, but potentially more devastating, postwildfire debris-flow scenario. The current (2010) assessment evaluates only postwildfire debris flows, but substantial hazards from flash floods without debris flow may remain for many years after a wildfire. Elliott and others (2005) estimated that burned drainage basins are most vulnerable to increased flood flows during the first 4 to 6 years after a wildfire.

Larger, less frequent rainstorms than those considered in this study likely will produce even larger postwildfire debris flows. Some areas within the selected basins may have higher debris-flow probabilities than indicated in this report, and debris flows may not be produced in all basins during postwildfire rainfall. However, the estimates and maps in this report can be used to prioritize areas within the basins or downstream from the basin outlets where emergency flood warnings or erosion mitigation may be needed for public safety.

The FLO-2D inundation modeling presented in this report is based on the 10-meter DEM, which indicates that the debris flows from Raspberry and Milton Creeks might converge to form one large debris-flow fan. Field evidence observed by Rold and Wright (1996), however, indicates that debris flows from Raspberry and Milton Creeks do not converge; therefore, the FLO-2D inundation maps presented in the current (2010) report might underestimate the easterly extent of the debris-flow inundation hazard.

This assessment is one perspective on debris-flow hazards in the Marble area and needs to be considered with other information as an indicator of potential risk. Historically the area near Marble has experienced periodic debris flows in the absence of wildfire, and this study only estimates the probability and volume of debris flow after wildfire. The postwildfire debris-flow model does not address the current (2010) prefire debris-flow hazards that exist near Marble, and new scientific information may indicate a need to revise current thinking about debris-flow hazards near Marble. The assessment is provided on the condition that neither the U.S. Geological Survey

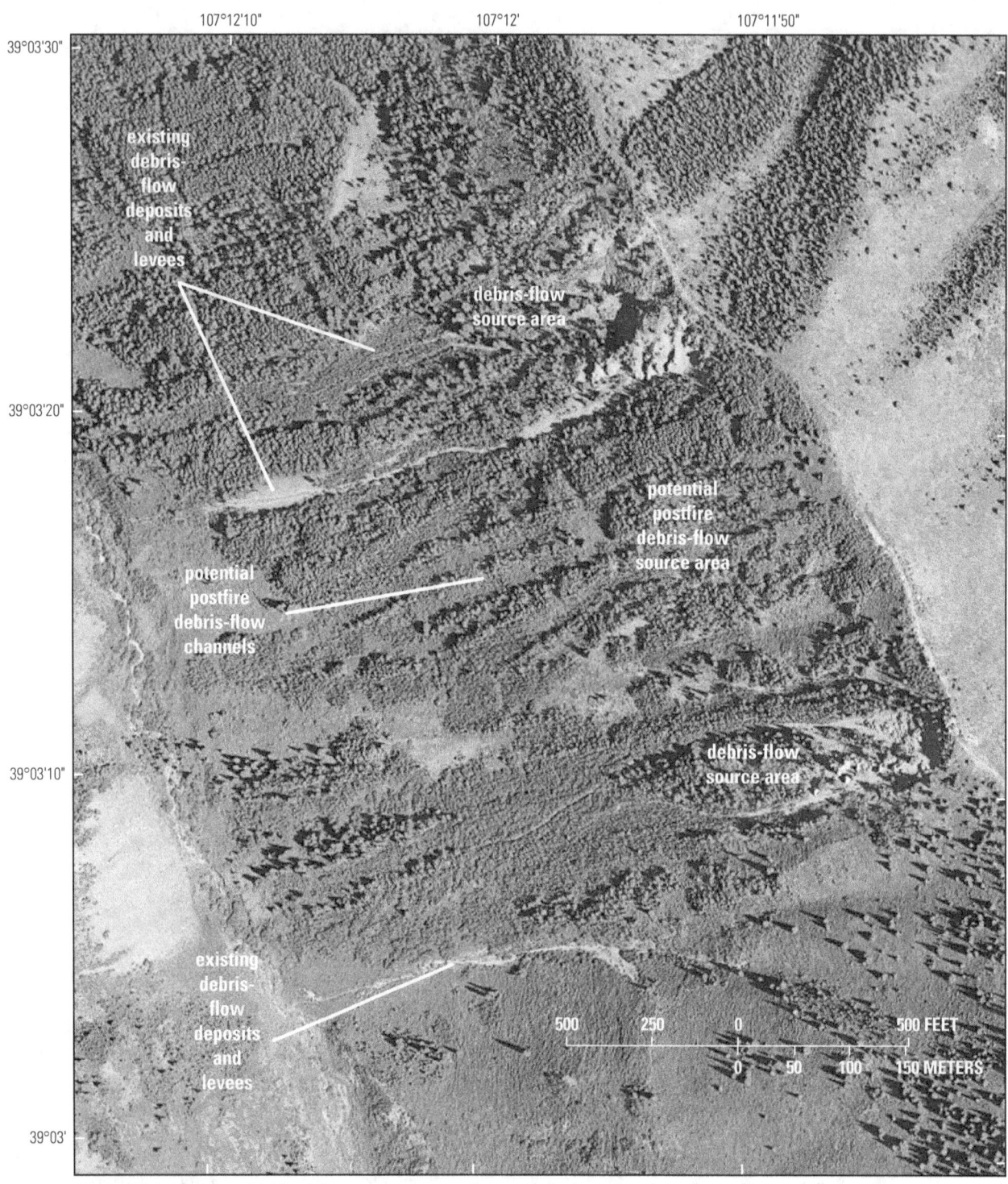

Base from U.S. Geological Survey digital data, 2009
National Agriculture Imagery Program
Universal Transverse Mercator projection, Zone 13

**Figure 19.**   Debris-flow source area and an incised channel lined by debris-flow levees in the Raspberry Creek drainage basin surrounded by forest that could burn in a wildfire (National Agriculture Imagery Program image, URL: http://datagateway.nrcs.usda.gov/).

**Figure 20.**   Channel of Milton Creek in June 2008, on a debris-flow fan showing large amounts of unsorted material available for entrainment by debris flows (Photograph taken by Mike Stevens, U.S. Geological Survey).

**Figure 21.**   Milton Creek at the confluence with the Crystal River where debris-flow material may potentially block the river and cause additional flooding, June 2008 (Photograph taken by Mike Stevens, U.S. Geological Survey).

**Figure 22.** Heavy equipment poised to unblock the stream channel near a bridge in a subdivision on the Milton Creek debris-flow fan near the confluence with the Crystal River, June 2008 (Photograph taken by Mike Stevens, U.S. Geological Survey).

**Figure 23.** Channel of Raspberry Creek in June 2008 showing debris-flow material available for possible entrainment in the future. U.S. Geological Survey topographic maps indicate that historically Raspberry and Milton Creeks converged upstream to form a single stream that flowed into the Crystal River. In 2010, the streams flow separately into the Crystal River (Photograph taken by Mike Stevens, U.S. Geological Survey).

nor the United States Government may be held liable for any damages resulting from the authorized or unauthorized use of the assessment.

# Summary

During 2009, the U.S. Geological Survey (USGS), in cooperation with Gunnison County, initiated a predictive study to estimate the potential for postwildfire debris flows to occur in the drainage basins occupied by Carbonate, Slate, Raspberry, and Milton Creeks near Marble, Colorado. Currently (2010), these drainage basins are unburned but could be burned by a future wildfire. This report provides estimates of probabilities of debris-flow occurrence and the debris-flow volumes that could be generated from Carbonate, Slate, Raspberry, and Milton Creek drainage basins in response to a wildfire that burns all areas vegetated with forest and shrubs at moderate- to high-burn severity and two hypothetical post-wildfire rainfalls of differing intensities. Debris-flow hydro-graphs defined for the estimated volumes are used as input to a model that estimates the areas inundated by debris-flow material beyond the outlets of each drainage basin. Results from a field reconnaissance of the Marble area to inspect debris-flow evidence and debris-flow source areas are described. Using the information provided in this report, land and water-supply managers can consider where to concentrate prewildfire planning. If a wildfire happens in the future, this information will help managers identify the drainage basins that are most vulnerable to postwildfire debris-flow hazards, and the areas that could be affected by debris flows.

Empirical models derived from statistical evaluation of data collected from postwildfire debris-flow sites throughout the intermountain western United States were used to estimate postwildfire probability and volumes of debris flows. Input for the postwildfire debris-flow models includes drainage basin area; area burned and burn severity; percentage of burned area; soil properties; rainfall total and intensity for the 5- and 25-year-recurrence, 1-hour-duration-rainfall; and topographic and soil property characteristics of the drainage basins occupied by the 4 creeks.

In this study, the debris-flow probability and volume estimates also were determined along the drainage network (existing flow paths or channels) using a continuous param-eterization technique. This technique was developed as an alternative to traditional basin characterization approaches, which require the selection of outlets and their corresponding basins using scientific knowledge or iterative analysis. The continuous parameterization technique also can facilitate the identification of smaller basins, with high probabilities for debris flow, within a larger basin. The continuous parameter-ization technique, based on a digital elevation model-derived flow-direction matrix, also facilitates faster parameter char-acterization and adds the capability to characterize basin ele-ments above any location, not just at the major drainage-basin outlets, which provides added detail.

Postwildfire rainfalls are a key variable used in the models that predict postwildfire debris-flow hazards. In this study, the hydrologic response to a 5-year-recurrence, 1-hour-duration rainfall of 23 millimeters, and a 25-year-recurrence, 1-hour-duration rainfall of 35 millimeters was evaluated. A 5-year-recurrence rainfall has a 20 percent chance of occurring in any given year, and a 25-year-recurrence rainfall has a 4 percent chance of occurring in any given year.

The estimated postwildfire debris-flow probabilities at the outlets of the 4 drainage basins ranged from 1 to 19 percent in response to the 5-year-recurrence, 1-hour duration rainfall, and from 3 to 35 percent in response to the 25-year-recurrence, 1-hour-duration rainfall. The largest probabilities of postwildfire debris flows are estimated for Raspberry Creek (19 and 35 percent), whereas estimated probabilities estimated for Carbonate, Slate, and Milton Creeks ranged from 1 to 6 percent. Of the four drainage basins, Raspberry Creek con-tains the most forest and shrub as a percentage of basin area; and therefore, the largest percent of potential burned area. The debris-flow probability model indicates that the 25-year-recurrence, 1-hour-duration rainfall debris-flow probabilities are 2 to 3 times higher than those for the 5-year-recurrence, 1-hour-duration rainfall.

When the postwildfire debris-flow probability model was implemented continuously along the drainage basin stream networks, many stream channels within the four drainage basins show debris-flow probabilities greater than 10 per-cent, and a few channels in the Raspberry Creek drainage basin show debris-flow probabilities greater than 40 percent, which indicates that some stream reaches within the basin are more susceptible to postwildfire debris flow than others. As expected, the estimated postwildfire debris-flow prob-abilities were greater in response to the 25-year-recurrence, 1-hour-duration rainfall than to the 5-year-recurrence, 1-hour-duration rainfall. In the Carbonate, Slate, and Milton Creek drainage basins, only a few locations in each basin indicated probabilities greater than 10 percent in response to either the 5- or 25-year-recurrence, 1-hour-duration rainfall. Results for the Raspberry Creek drainage basin, considering the 25-year-recurrence, 1-hour-duration rainfall, indicate widespread areas with probabilities of postwildfire debris-flow greater than 10 percent, and many areas with probabilities greater than 20 percent.

Debris-flow volumes estimated at the outlet of the 4 drainage basins for the 5- and 25-year-recurrence, 1-hour-duration rainfalls are, respectively, Carbonate Creek 101,000 and 126,000 m$^3$; Slate Creek 7,500 and 9,400 m$^3$; Raspberry Creek 59,000 and 74,000 m$^3$; and Milton Creek 100,000 and 125,000 m$^3$. Carbonate Creek and Milton Creek had the larg-est estimated volumes. The results indicate that the 25-year-recurrence, 1-hour-duration rainfall increases postwildfire debris-flow volume at the four drainage basin outlets by about 25 percent compared to the 5-year-recurrence, 1-hour-duration rainfall.

Postwildfire debris-flow volumes also were estimated using the continuous parameterization technique. The results for the four drainage basins generally indicate that the volume of water and sediment increased as contributing drainage area increased. Because all the coefficients for the variables in the model are positive, and burned area (potentially the strongest variable in the equation) never decreases as contributing drainage area is added in the downstream direction, hence progressively larger postwildfire debris-flow volumes are estimated in the downstream direction.

Results from the quasi-two-dimensional floodplain computer model (FLO-2D) of the 5-year-recurrence, 1-hour-duration rainfall indicate that postwildfire debris flows from Carbonate, Raspberry, and Milton Creeks would flow to the Crystal River, and the debris flow in Slate Creek would nearly reach the river. In response to the 25-year-recurrence, 1-hour-duration rainfall the postwildfire debris flow from the Carbonate, Raspberry, Slate, and Milton Creek drainage basins were estimated to all reach the Crystal River. Comparing results of the 5- and 25-year-recurrence interval, 1-hour-duration rainfalls, only small differences in the inundation areas and depths of debris-flow material were estimated by the FLO-2D model. There is much uncertainty with respect to the postwildfire debris-flow hazards associated with larger storm events than were considered in this study, such as the 100-year-recurrence rainfall, and caution is needed.

Estimated postwildfire debris-flow materials exceeded a depth of 5 meters in some areas. Comparing the FLO-2D modeling inundation results of the 5- and 25-year-recurrence, 1-hour-duration rainfalls, only small differences in the inundation areas and depths of debris-flow material were estimated. Existing stream channels or topographic flow paths seem to control the distribution of debris-flow material, and the difference in estimated debris-flow volume (about 25 percent more volume for the 25-year-recurrence, 1-hour-duration rainfall compared to the 5-year-recurrence, 1-hour-duration rainfall) does not seem to substantially affect the estimated spatial distribution of debris-flow material.

Predicted maximum instantaneous depths of debris-flow material along the channel of the Crystal River need to be considered coarse estimates because the dilution of the debris-flow material from the river was not simulated by the FLO-2D model, and less concentrated mixtures could exhibit different behavior. Also, blockages by coarse debris such as trees, houses, vehicles, and large boulders might alter the flow paths of any of the predicted debris flows or the channel of the Crystal River, and these possible affects were not modeled.

Historically the Marble area has experienced periodic debris flows in the absence of wildfire. This report estimates the probability and volume of debris flow and maximum instantaneous inundation area depths after hypothetical wildfire and rainfall. This postwildfire debris-flow report does not address the current (2010) prewildfire debris-flow hazards that exist near Marble. The assessment is provided on the condition that neither the U.S. Geological Survey nor the United States Government may be held liable for any damages resulting from the authorized or unauthorized use of the assessment.

# Acknowledgments

The author gratefully acknowledges the useful insights provided by Richard Stenson, Environmental Health Official, Gunnison County Department of Planning, Building, and Environmental Health, and critical reviews by Susan Cannon and John Elliott, USGS.

# References

Bertolo, P., and Wieczorek, G.F., 2005, Calibration of numerical models for small debris flows in Yosemite Valley, California, USA: Natural Hazards and Earth System Sciences, v. 5, p. 993–1001.

Cannon, S.H., Gartner, J.E., and Michael, J.A., 2007, Methods for the emergency assessment of debris-flow hazards from basins burned by the fires of 2007, southern California: U.S. Geological Survey Open-File Report 2007–1384, 10 p.

Cannon, S.H., Gartner, J.E., Rupert, M.G., Michael, J.A., Rea, A.H., and Parrett, C., 2010, Predicting the probability and volume of postwildfire debris flows in the intermountain western United States: Geological Society of America Bulletin, v. 122, p. 127–144.

Cannon, S.H., Gartner, J.E., Wilson, R.C., and Laber, J.L., 2008, Storm rainfall conditions for floods and debris flows from recently burned areas in southwestern Colorado and southern California: Geomorphology, v. 96, p. 250–269.

Cannon, S.H., Gartner, J.E., and Michael, J.A., 2007, Methods for the emergency assessment of debris-flow hazards from basins burned by the fires of 2007, southern California: U.S. Geological Survey Open-File Report 2007–1384, 10 p.

Cerrelli, G.A., 2005, FIRE HYDRO, a simplified method for predicting peak discharges to assist in the design of flood protection measures for western wildfires, in Moglen, G.E., ed., Proceedings: 2005 watershed management conference—managing watersheds for human and natural impacts: engineering, ecological, and economic challenges, July 19–22, 2005, Williamsburg, Va.: Alexandria, Va., American Society of Civil Engineers, p. 935–941.

Costa, J.E., 1988, Rheologic, geomorphic, and sedimentologic differentiation of water floods, hyperconcentrated flows, and debris flows, in Flood geomorphology: New York, John Wiley and Sons, p. 113–122.

Costa, J.E., and Jarrett, R.D., 1981, Debris flows in small mountain stream channels of Colorado and their hydrologic implications: Bulletin of the Association of Engineering Geologists, v. XVIII, no. 3, p. 309–322.

Das, B.M., 1983, Advanced soil mechanics: New York, McGraw-Hill, 511 p.

Elliott, J.G., Flynn, J.L., Bossong, C.R., and Char, S.J., 2011, Estimated probabilities and volumes of postwildfire debris flows, a prewildfire evaluation for the upper Blue River watershed, Summit County, Colorado: U.S. Geological Survey Scientific Investigations Report 2011–5039, 22 p.

Elliott, J.G., Smith, M.E., Friedel, M.J., Stevens, M.R., Bossong, C.R., Litke, D.W., Parker, R.S., Costello, C., Wagner, J., Char, S.J., Bauer, M.A., and Wilds, S.R., 2005, Analysis and mapping of post-fire hydrologic hazards for the 2002 Hayman, Coal Seam, and Missionary Ridge wildfires, Colorado: U.S. Geological Survey Scientific Investigations Report 2004–5300, 104 p.

Elverhoi, A., Harbitz, C.B., Dimakis, P., Mohrig, D., Marr, J., and Parker, G., 2000, On the dynamics of subaqueous debris flows: Oceanography, v. 13, no. 3, p. 109–117.

Enos, P., 1977, Flow regimes in debris flow: Sedimentology, v. 24, p. 133–142.

ESRI, 2009, ArcGIS version 9.3: Redlands, Calif., ESRI.

Gartner, J.E., Cannon, S.H., Santi, P.M., and DeWolfe, V.G., 2008, Empirical models to predict debris-flow volumes generated from recently burned basins in the western U.S.: Geomorphology, v. 96, p. 339–354.

Gaskill, D.L., and Godwin, L.H., 1966, Geologic map of the Marble quadrangle, Gunnison and Pitkin counties: U.S. Geological Survey Geologic Quadrangle Map GQ-512.

Gesch, D., Oimoen, M., Greenlee, S., Nelson, C., Steuck, M., and Tyler, D., 2002, The national elevation dataset: Photogrammetric Engineering and Remote Sensing, v. 68, no. 1, p. 5–11.

Grove, M., Harbor, J., and Engel, B., 1998, Composite vs. distributed curve numbers—effects on estimates of storm runoff depths: Journal of the American Water Resources Association. v. 34, no. 5, p. 1015–1023.

Helsel, D.R., and Hirsch, R.M., 1992, Statistical methods in water resources: New York, Elsevier Studies in Environmental Science, v. 49, 529 p.

Homer, C., Dewitz, J., Fry, J., Coan, M., Hossain, N., Larson, C., Herold, N., McKerrow, A., VanDriel, J.K., and Wickham, J., 2007, Completion of the 2001 national land cover database for the conterminous United States: Photogrammetric Engineering and Remote Sensing, v. 73, no. 4, p. 337–341.

Hosmer, D.W., and Lemeshow, S., 2000, Applied logistic regression, 2nd edition: New York, John Wiley & Sons, Inc., 375 p.

International Atomic Energy Agency (IAEA), 2008, Field estimation of soil water content: IAEA Training Course Series No. 30, 131 p.

Istanbulluoglu, E., Tarboton, D.G., Pack, R.T., and Luce, C.H., 2004, Modeling of the interactions between forest vegetation, disturbances, and sediment yields: Journal of Geophysical Research, v. 109, F01009, doi:10.1029/2003JF000041, 22 p.

Kaitna, R., Rickenmann, D., and Schatzmann, M., 2007, Experimental study on rheologic behavior of debris-flow material: Acta Geotechnica, v. 2, no. 2, p. 71–85.

Keane, R.E., Ryan, K.C., Veblen, T.T., Allen, C.D., Logan, J., and Hawkes, B., 2002, Cascading effects of fire exclusion in the Rocky Mountain ecosystems—a literature review: U.S. Department of Agriculture, Forest Service, Rocky Mountain Research Station General Technical Report RMRS-GTR-91, 24 p.

Lindsey, Rebecca, 2002, Satellites aid burn area rehabilitation: National Aeronautic and Space Administration online report, various pagination, available at *http:// earthobservatory.nasa.gov/Study/BAER/printall.php*

Livingston, R.K., Earles, T.A., Wright, K.R., 2005, Los Alamos post-fire watershed recovery: a curve-number-based evaluation, *in* Moglen, G.E., eds., Proceedings: 2005 watershed management conference-managing watersheds for human and natural impacts: engineering, ecological, and economic challenges; July 19–22, 2005, Williamsburg, Va.: Alexandria, Va., American Society of Civil Engineers, p. 471–481.

Melton, M.A., 1965, The geomorphic and paleoclimate significance of alluvial deposits in southern Arizona: Journal of Geology, v. 73, p. 1–38.

Miller, J.F., Frederick, R.H., and Tracey, R.J., 1973, Precipitation-frequency atlas of the western United States, v. 3—Colorado: Silver Spring, Md., U.S. Department of Commerce, National Oceanic and Atmospheric Administration, National Weather Service, Atlas 2.

O'Brien, J., 2009, FLO-2D Reference manual, version 2009: Nutrioso, Arizona, FLO-2D Software Inc., 63 p.

O'Brien, J.S., and Julien, P.Y., 1988, Laboratory analysis of mudflow properties: Journal of Hydraulic Engineering, v. 114, no. 8, p. 877–887.

Pierson, T.C., and Costa, J.E., 1987, A rheologic classification of subaerial sediment-water flows: Geological Society of America, Reviews in Engineering Geology, v. VII, 12 p.

Pierson, T.C., and Scott, K.M., 1985, Downstream dilution of a lahar; Transition from debris flow to hyperconcentrated streamflow: Water Resources Research, v. 21, p. 1511–1524.

Ponce, V.M., and Hawkins, R.H., 1996, Runoff curve number—Has it reached maturity?: Journal of Hydrologic Engineering, v. 1, no. 1, p. 11–19.

Rogers, W.P., and Rold, J.W., 1972, Engineering geologic factors of the Marble area, Gunnison County, Colorado: Colorado Geological Survey Miscellaneous Report No. 8, 45 p.

Rold, J.W., 1977, The Marble area, a development frontier *in* Veal, H.K. ed., Exploration frontiers of the central and southern Rockies: Rocky Mountain Association of Geologists, 1977 Symposium, Denver, Colorado, p. 427–439.

Rold, J.W., and Wright, K.R., 1996, Geologic and hydrologic factors governing impacts of development on the Crystal River near Marble, Gunnison County, Colorado: Denver, Colorado, Wright Water Engineers, Inc., Job number 951-110.000, 67 p. URL: *http://www.gunnisoncounty.org/planning_pdf/Marble_Report.pdf*

Ruddy, B.C., Stevens, M.R., Verdin, K.L., and Elliott, J.G., 2010, Probability and volume of potential postwildfire debris flows in the 2010 Fourmile burn area, Boulder County, Colorado: U.S. Geological Survey Open-File Report 2010–1244. 5 p.

Rupert, M.G., Cannon, S.H., Gartner, J.E., Michael, J.A., and Helsel, D.R., 2008, Using logistic regression to predict the probability of debris flows in areas burned by wildfires, southern California, 2003–2006: U.S. Geological Survey Open-File Report 2008–1370, 20 p.

Schwartz, G.E., and Alexander, R.B., 1995, State Soil Geographic (STATSGO) data base for the conterminous United States: U.S. Geological Survey Open-File Report 95–449.

Sen, Z., 2008, Instantaneous runoff coefficient variation and peak discharge estimation model: Journal of Hydrologic Engineering, April 2008, p. 270–277.

Simons, Li & Associates, Inc., 1983, Hydrology report for Town of Rangely, City of Rifle and Garfield County flood insurance studies: Denver, Colorado, FEMA Contract No. EMW-C-0942, variously paginated.

Springer, E.P., and Hawkins, R.H., 2005, Curve number and peakflow responses following the Cerro Grande Fire on a small watershed, *in* Moglen, G.E., eds., Proceedings: 2005 watershed management conference-managing watersheds for human and natural impacts: engineering, ecological, and economic challenges; July 19–22, 2005, Williamsburg, Va.: Alexandria, Va., American Society of Civil Engineers, p. 459–470.

SPSS, Inc., 2000, SYSTAT 10, Statistics I–Software documentation: Chicago, SPSS, Inc., 663 p.

Stevens, M.R., Bossong, C.R., Litke, D.W., Viger, R.J., Rupert, M.G., and Char, S.J., 2008, Estimated probability of postwildfire debris-flow occurrence and estimated volume of debris flows from a pre-fire analysis in the Three Lakes Watershed, Grand County, Colorado: U.S. Geological Survey Scientific Investigations Map 3009, 1 sheet.

U.S. Army Corps of Engineers, 2001, Hydrologic modeling system HEC-HMS: Davis, Calif., U.S. Army Corps of Engineers Hydrologic Engineering Center, 188 p.

U.S. Department of Agriculture, 1986, Urban hydrology for small watersheds (2nd ed.): Natural Resources Conservation Service Technical Release 55 (TR-55), 164 p.

U.S. Department of Agriculture, National Resources Conservation Service, National Soil Survey Center, 1991, State Soil Geographic (STATSGO) database:  Data use information, Miscellaneous Publication Number 1492, 110 p. (Revised July 1994)

Verdin, K.L. and Greenlee, S., 2003, Continuous parameterization using EDNA, *in* Proceedings of the 2003 ESRI User's Conference, July 7–11, 2003, San Diego, Calif., accessed May 2007 at *http://gis.esri.com/library/userconf/proc03/p0617.pdf.*

Verdin, K.L., and Worstell, B., 2008, A fully distributed implementation of mean annual streamflow regional regression equations: Journal of the American Water Resources Association, v. 44, p. 1537–1547. doi: 10.1111/j.1752-1688.2008.00258.x

Wood, M.K., and Blackburn, W.H., 1984, An evaluation of the hydrologic soil groups as used in the SCS runoff method on rangelands: Water Resources Bulletin, v. 20, no. 3, p. 379–389.